Stand Out

Standards-Based English

4

Staci Lyn Sabbagh

Rob Jenkins

THOMSON
HEINLE

Australia • Canada • Mexico • Singapore • Spain • United Kingdom • United States

THOMSON

HEINLE

Stand Out 4
Standards-Based English

Staci Lyn Sabbagh and Rob Jenkins

Acquisitions Editor
Sherrise Roehr

Managing Editor
James W. Brown

Developmental Editor
Ingrid Wisniewska

Associate Developmental Editor
Sarah Barnicle

Editorial Assistant
Elizabeth Allen

Marketing Manager
Eric Bredenberg

Director, Global ESL Training & Development
Evelyn Nelson

Production Editor
Jeff Freeland

Senior Manufacturing Coordinator
Mary Beth Hennebury

Photo Researcher
Sheri Blaney

Project Manager
Carole Rollins

Compositor
TSI Graphics

Text Printer/Binder
Banta

Cover Printer
Phoenix Color Corporation

Designers
Elise Kaiser
Julia Gecha

Cover Designer
Gina Petti

Illustrators
James Edwards represented by Sheryl Beranbaum
Vilma Ortiz-Dillon
Scott MacNeill

Cover Art
Diana Ong/SuperStock

For more information, contact Heinle Publishers, 25 Thomson Place, Boston, MA 02210; or find us on the World Wide Web at: www.heinle.com

For permission to use material from this text or product, contact us by:
Tel   1-800-730-2214
Fax   1-800-730-2215
www.thomsonrights.com

Library of Congress Catalog-in-Publication Data

Sabbagh, Staci Lyn.
  Stand out 4 : standards-based English /
  Staci Lyn Sabbagh, Rob Jenkins.
    p. cm.
  Includes index.
  ISBN 0-8384-2236-5
    1. English language—Textbooks for foreign
    speakers. I. Title: Stand out four. II.
  Jenkins, Rob. III. Title.

  PE1128 .S214 2002
  428.2'4—dc21

2002068463

CREDITS

PHOTO CREDITS

Page v: Courtney Sabbagh

Unit 1:
Page 1: left: Dion Ogust/The Image Works; right: David Young-Wolff/Photo Edit
Page 3: top: Dean Berry/Index Stock Imagery; bottom: Grantpix/Index Stock Imagery
Page 6: Bill Lai/Index Stock Imagery
Page 9: top left: Bill Lai/Index Stock Imagery; center: Myrleen Cate/Index Stock Imagery; bottom left: Benelux Press/Index Stock Imagery; bottom right: David Young-Wolff/Photo Edit
Page 12: left: Jeff Greenberg/Photo Edit; center: Jeff Dunn/Index Stock Imagery; right: Comstock RF
Page 13 Myrleen Cate/Photo Edit

Unit 2:
Page 24: top: Comstock RF; 2nd from top: Jean Coughlin; 3rd from top: Comstock RF; bottom: Jean Coughlin
Page 26: Michael Keller/Index Stock Imagery

Unit 3:
Page 41: left: Gay Bumgarner/Index Stock Imagery; center: Carl/Joan Vanderschuit/Index Stock Imagery; right: Omni Photo Communications/Index Stock Imagery
Page 43: top: Carl/Joan Vanderschuit/Index Stock Imagery; bottom: Omni Photo Communications/Index Stock Imagery
Page 47: left: John Connell/Index Stock Imagery; center left: Wendell Metzen/Index Stock Imagery; center right: John Connell/Index Stock Imagery; right: Gay Bumgarner/Index Stock Imagery
Page 57: top left: Wendell Metzen/Index Stock Imagery; center: John Connell/Index Stock Imagery; bottom left: Gay Bumgarner/Index Stock Imagery

Unit 4:
Page 63: Bill Aron/Photo Edit
Page 75: top: Robert Ginn/Index Stock Imagery; 2nd from top: Thomas Craig/Index Stock Imagery; 3rd from top: Diaphor/Index Stock Imagery; bottom: Jeff Greenberg/Photo Edit

Unit 5:
Page 81: left: Myrleen Cate/Index Stock Imagery; center left: Steve Dunwell/Index Stock Imagery; center right: Chip Henderson/Index Stock Imagery; right: David Young-Wolff/Photo Edit

Unit 6:
Page 102: top: Digital Vision RF/Picture Quest; 2nd from top: Jeff Greenberg/Photo Edit; 3rd from top: Scott Witte/Index Stock Imagery; bottom: Diaphor Agency/Index Stock Imagery
Page 105: Richard Lord/The Image Works
Page 107: Spencer Grant/Photo Edit
Page 114: Spencer Grant/Photo Edit

Unit 7:
Page 122: left: Michelle D. Bridwell/Photo Edit; right: Myrleen Ferguson Cate/Photo Edit
Page 125: Dana White/Photo Edit
Page 135: Michael Newman/Photo Edit
Page 145: John Neubauer/Photo Edit

Unit 8:
Page 152: top left: Asami Haseqawa/Index Stock Imagery; top right: Jose Azel/AURORA; bottom left: David Rosenberg/Index Stock Imagery; bottom right: Spencer Ainsley/The Image Works
Page 154: top: Rob Bartee/Index Stock Imagery; center: Larry George/Index Stock Imagery; bottom: Peter Walton/Index Stock Imagery
Page 155: Peter Walton/Index Stock Imagery

TEXT CREDITS

Pages 17, 58, and 96: Special thanks to Kate Kinsella of San Francisco State University for permission to use her ideas on vocabulary cards and tips for writing summaries.
Page 23: Information on how to be a smart consumer adapted from www.ftc.gov, web site of the Federal Trade Commission.
Page 28: Article on how to choose a credit card adapted with permission from www.creditcardmenu.com, a service of Gromco Inc.
Pages 53 and 54: Statistics on Homeownership in the United States from U.S. Census Bureau, Current Population Survey.
Page 68: Information on public library services adapted with permission from Coronado Public Library, Coronado CA.
Page 88: Medical insurance application adapted with permission from Allen Insurance, http://www.allenins.com
Page 91: Text on reading nutrition labels adapted with permission from Physicians Wellness Network Ltd. (PWNLTD.com).
Page 94: Article on the common cold adapted from information prepared by The National Institute of Allergy and Infectious Diseases, National Institute of Health, U.S. Department of Health and Human Services, www.niaid.nih.gov/factsheets/cold.htm
Page 132: Article on 'How to Ask for a Raise' adapted with permission from Business and Professional Women/USA, http://www.bpwusa.org.
Page 146: Jury summons adapted with permission from Metropolitan Government of Nashville & Davidson County, www.nashville.gov
Pages 147, 148, and 149: Income tax forms from The Internal Revenue Service, Department of the Treasury

ACKNOWLEDGMENTS

The authors and publisher would like to thank the following reviewers, consultants, and participants in focus groups:

Elizabeth Aderman
New York City Board of Education, New York, NY

Sharon Baker
Roseville Adult School, Roseville, CA

Shannon Bailey
Austin Community College, Austin, TX

Lillian Barredo
Stockton School for Adults, Stockton, CA

Linda Boice
Elk Grove Adult Education, Elk Grove, CA

Rose Cantu
John Jay High School Adult Education, San Antonio, TX

Toni Chapralis
Fremont School for Adults, Sacramento, CA

Melanie Chitwood
Miami-Dade Community College, Miami, FL

Geri Creamer
Stockton School for Adults, Stockton, CA

Irene Dennis
San Antonio College, San Antonio, TX

Eileen Duffell
P.S. 64, New York, NY

Nancy Dunlap
Northside Independent School District, San Antonio, TX

Gloria Eriksson
Old Marshall Adult Education Center, Sacramento, CA

Marti Estrin
Santa Rosa Junior College, Santa Rosa, CA

Judith Finkelstein
Reseda Community Adult School, Reseda, CA

Lawrence Fish
Shorefront YM-YWHA English Language Program, Brooklyn, NY

Victoria Florit
Miami-Dade Community College, Miami, FL

Kathleen Flynn
Glendale Community College, Glendale, CA

Rhoda Gilbert
New York City Board of Education, New York, NY

Kathleen Jimenez
Miami-Dade Community College, Miami, FL

Nancy Jordan
John Jay High School Adult Education, San Antonio, TX

Renee Klosz
Lindsey Hopkins Technical Education Center, Miami, FL

David Lauter
Stockton School for Adults, Stockton, CA

Patricia Long
Old Marshall Adult Education Center, Sacramento, CA

Maria Miranda
Lindsey Hopkins Technical Education Center, Miami, FL

Karen Moore
Stockton School for Adults, Stockton, CA

Erin Nyhan
Triton College, Chicago, IL

Marta Pitt
Lindsey Hopkins Technical Education Center, Miami, FL

Sylvia Rambach
Stockton School for Adults, Stockton, CA

Myra Redman
Miami-Dade Community College, Miami, FL

Charleen Richardson
San Antonio College, San Antonio, TX

Eric Rosenbaum
Bronx Community College, New York, NY

Laura Rowley
Old Marshall Adult Education Center, Sacramento, CA

Sr. M. B. Theresa Spittle
Stockton School for Adults, Stockton, CA

Andre Sutton
Belmont Adult School, Belmont, CA

Jennifer Swoyer
Northside Independent School District, San Antonio, TX

Claire Valier
Palm Beach County School District, West Palm Beach, FL

The authors would like to thank Joel and Rosanne for believing in us, Eric for seeing our vision, Nancy and Sherrise for going to bat for us, and Jim, Ingrid, and Sarah for making the book a reality.

Rob Jenkins

I love teaching. I love to see the expressions on my students' faces when the light goes on and their eyes show such sincere joy of learning. I knew the first time I stepped into an ESL classroom that this was where I needed to be and I have never questioned that resolution. I have worked in business, sales, and publishing, and I've found challenge in all, but nothing can compare to the satisfaction of reaching people in such a personal way.

Thanks to my family who have put up with late hours and early mornings, my friends at church who support me, and all the people at Santa Ana College, School of Continuing Education who believe in me and are a source of tremendous inspiration.

Staci Lyn Sabbagh

Ever since I can remember, I've been fascinated with other cultures and languages. I love to travel and every place I go, the first thing I want to do is meet the people, learn their language, and understand their culture. Becoming an ESL teacher was a perfect way to turn what I love to do into my profession. There's nothing more incredible than the exchange of teaching and learning from one another that goes on in an ESL classroom. And there's nothing more rewarding than helping a student succeed.

I would especially like to thank Mom, Dad, CJ, Tete, Eric, my close friends and my Santa Ana College, School of Continuing Education family. Your love and support inspired me to do something I never imagined I could. And Rob, thank you for trusting me to be part of such an amazing project.

We are lesson plan enthusiasts! We have learned that good lesson planning makes for effective teaching and, more importantly, good learning. We also believe that learning is stimulated by task-oriented activities in which students find themselves critically laboring over decisions and negotiating meaning from their own personal perspectives.

The need to write **Stand Out** came to us as we were leading a series of teacher workshops on project-based simulations designed to help students apply what they have learned. We began to teach lesson planning within our workshops in order to help teachers see how they could incorporate the activities more effectively. Even though teachers showed great interest in both the projects and planning, they often complained that lesson planning took too much time that they simply didn't have. Another obstacle was that the books available to the instructors were not conducive to planning lessons.

We decided to write our own materials by first writing lesson plans that met specific student-performance objectives. Then we developed the student pages that were needed to make the lesson plans work in the classroom. The student book only came together after the plans! Writing over 300 lesson plans has been a tremendous challenge and has helped us evaluate our own teaching and approach. It is our hope that others will discover the benefits of always following a plan in the classroom and incorporating the strategies we have included in these materials.

ABOUT THE SERIES

The **Stand Out** series is designed to facilitate *active* learning while challenging students to build a nurturing and effective learning community.

The student books are divided into eight distinct units, mirroring competency areas most useful to newcomers. These areas are outlined in CASAS assessment programs and different state model standards for adults. Each unit is then divided into eight lessons and a team project activity. Lessons are driven by performance objectives and are filled with challenging activities that progress from teacher-presented to student-centered tasks.

SUPPLEMENTAL MATERIALS

- The *Stand Out Lesson Planner* is in full color with 77 complete lesson plans, taking the instructor through each stage of a lesson from warm-up and review through application.

- The *Activity Bank CD-ROM* has an abundance of materials, some of which are customizable. Print or download and modify what you need for your particular class.

- The *Stand Out Grammar Challenge* is a workbook that gives additional grammar explanation and practice.

- The *Stand Out* ExamView® Pro *Test Bank CD-ROM* allows you to customize pre- and posttests for each unit as well as a pre- and posttest for the book.

- **The listening scripts** are found in the back of the student book and the Lesson Planner. Cassette tapes and CD-ROMs are available with focused listening activities described in the Lesson Planner.

STAND OUT LESSON PLANNER

The *Stand Out Lesson Planner* is a new and innovative approach. As many seasoned teachers know, good lesson planning can make a substantial difference in the classroom. Students continue coming to class, understanding, applying, and remembering more of what they learn. They are more confident in their learning when good lesson planning techniques are incorporated.

We have developed lesson plans that are designed to be used each day and to reduce preparation time. The planner includes:

- Standard lesson progression (Warm-up and Review, Introduction, Presentation, Practice, Evaluation, and Application)

- A creative and complete way to approach varied class lengths so that each lesson will work within a class period.

- 231 hours of classroom activities

- Time suggestions for each activity

- Pedagogical comments

- Space for teacher notes and future planning

- Identification of SCANS, EFF, and CASAS standards

USER QUESTIONS ABOUT STAND OUT

- **What are SCANS and EFF and how do they integrate into the book?**
  SCANS is the **S**ecretary's **C**ommission on **A**cquiring **N**ecessary **S**kills. SCANS was developed to encourage students to prepare for the workplace. The standards developed through SCANS have been incorporated throughout the **Stand Out** student books and components.

  Stand Out addresses SCANS a little differently than other books. SCANS standards elicit effective teaching strategies by incorporating essential skills such as critical thinking and group work. We have incorporated SCANS standards in every lesson, not isolating these standards in the work unit, as is typically done.

  EFF, or **E**quipped **f**or the **F**uture, is another set of standards established to address students' roles as parents, workers, and citizens, with a vision of student literacy and lifelong learning. **Stand Out** addresses these standards and integrates them into the materials in a similar way to SCANS.

- **What about CASAS?** The federal government has mandated that states show student outcomes as a prerequisite to funding. Some states have incorporated the **C**omprehensive **A**dult **S**tudent **A**ssessment **S**ystem (CASAS) testing to standardize agency reporting. Unfortunately, since many of our students are unfamiliar with standardized testing and therefore struggle with it, adult schools need to develop lesson plans to address specific concerns. **Stand Out** was developed with careful attention to CASAS skill areas in most lessons and performance objectives.

Are the tasks too challenging for my students?
Students learn by doing and learn more when challenged. **Stand Out** provides tasks that encourage critical thinking in a variety of ways. The tasks in each lesson move from teacher-directed to student-centered so the learner clearly understands what's expected and is willing to "take a risk." The lessons are expected to be challenging. In this way, students learn that when they work together as a learning community, anything becomes possible. The satisfaction of accomplishing something both as an individual and as a member of a team results in greater confidence and effective learning.

Do I need to understand lesson planning to teach from the student book? If you don't understand lesson planning when you start, you will when you finish! Teaching from **Stand Out** is like a course on lesson planning, especially if you use the Lesson Planner on a daily basis.

Stand Out does *stand out* because, when we developed this series, we first established performance objectives for each lesson. Then we designed lesson plans, followed by student book pages. The introduction to each lesson varies because different objectives demand different approaches. **Stand Out's** variety of tasks makes learning more interesting for the student.

What are team projects? The final lesson of each unit is a **team project.** This is often a team simulation that incorporates the objectives of the unit and provides an additional opportunity for students to actively apply what they have learned. The project allows students to produce something that represents their progress in learning. These end-of-unit projects were created with a variety of learning styles and individual skills in mind. The team projects can be skipped or simplified, but we encourage instructors to implement them, enriching the overall student experience.

What do you mean by a customizable Activity Bank? Every class, student, teacher, and approach is different. Since no one textbook can meet all these differences, the *Activity Bank CD-ROM* allows you to customize **Stand Out** for your class. You can copy different activities and worksheets from the CD-ROM to your hard drive and then:

- change items in supplemental vocabulary, grammar, and life skill activities;

- personalize activities with student names and popular locations in your area;

- extend every lesson with additional practice where you feel it is most needed.

Is this a grammar-based or a competency-based series? This is a competency-based series, with grammar identified more clearly and more boldly than in other similar series. We believe that grammar instruction in context is extremely important. Grammar structures are frequently identified as principal lesson objectives. Students are first provided with context that incorporates the grammar, followed by an explanation and practice. At this level, we expect students to acquire language structure after hearing and reading grammar in useful contexts. For teachers who want to enhance grammar instruction, the *Activity Bank CD-ROM* and/or the *Stand Out Grammar Challenge* workbooks provide ample opportunities.

The six competencies that drive **Stand Out** are basic communication, consumer economics, community resources, health, occupational knowledge, and lifelong learning (government and law replace lifelong learning in Books 3 and 4).

Are there enough activities so I don't have to supplement? Stand Out stands alone in providing 231 hours of instruction and activities, even without the additional suggestions in the Lesson Planner. The Lesson Planner also shows you how to streamline lessons to provide 115 hours of classwork and still have thorough lessons if you meet less often. When supplementing with the *Activity Bank CD-ROM,* the ExamView® *Test Bank CD-ROM,* and the *Stand Out Grammar Challenge* workbooks, you gain unlimited opportunities to extend class hours and provide activities related directly to each lesson objective. Calculate how many hours your class meets in a semester and look to **Stand Out** to address the full class experience.

Stand Out is a comprehensive approach to adult language learning, meeting needs of students and instructors completely and effectively.

CONTENTS

Theme	Unit and page number	Life Skills	Language Functions	Grammar	Vocabulary
Basic communication	**Pre-unit Getting to Know You** *Page P2*	• Fill out an admission application • Make life goals	• Introduce yourself • Introduce your friends	• Identify and correct different types of errors in written work	• Parts of a paragraph: *topic, support, and conclusion sentences* • Recognize word families • Parts of speech: *noun, verb, adjective, adverb*
Basic communication	**1 Balancing Your Life** *Page1*	• Make a goal chart • Analyze problems and come up with different possible solutions • Understand time management skills	• Compare past and present habits and states • Give and respond to advice • Discuss obstacles and solutions	• *Used to* for past habits and states—affirmative, negative, and question forms • *Can* or *could* to make suggestions • Restrictive adjective clauses with *where, who, that,* and *which*	• Careers and jobs: *architect, intern, partner, qualifications, retired* • Making goals: *achieve, goal, obstacle, solution* • Time management: *accomplish, allocate, deadlines, plan, prioritize, schedule*
Consumer economics	**2 Personal Finance** *Page 21*	• Discuss things to consider before making a large purchase • Interpret credit card information • Interpret loan information • Analyze advertising techniques	• Compare reasons for choosing different products • Describe problem situations • Express complaints	• Contrary-to-fact conditionals—affirmative, negative, and question forms	• Making a purchase: *discount, guarantee, pricing policy, refund, return, sale, warranty* • Using a credit card: *annual fee, APR, cash advance, credit limit, creditworthy, grace period, interest*
Consumer economics	**3 Buying a Home** *Page 41*	• Interpret housing advertisements • Use a housing preferences checklist • Write a letter to a real estate agent • Understand steps in the process of buying a home	• Compare different types of homes • Express preferences related to housing • Discuss and compare living in a house or a condominium	• Comparative and superlative adjectives • Questions with comparative and superlative adjectives • *Yes/no* and information questions	• Adjectives to describe housing: *cheap, comfortable, dark, noisy, safe, spacious* • Buying a home: *asking price, closing, contract, inspect, lender, negotiate, offer*
Community resources	**4 Community** *Page 61*	• Identify resources in a community • Read a community bulletin board • Identify and access library services • Interpret a road map • Volunteer in your community	• Ask for information about places in the community • Make and respond to suggestions • Give and understand road map directions • Describe skills needed for volunteer work • Interpret location/event descriptions	• Embedded question forms for *wh-* questions and *yes/no* questions • *Why don't we / Let's* + base form • *How about* + gerund	• Places in the community: *baseball league, clinic, court, DMV, senior center, summer camp* • Volunteer work: *build, keep track of, organize, plan, spend time with*

EFF	SCANS (Workplace)	Academic/Math	CASAS
Most EFF skills are incorporated into this unit, with an emphasis on: • Taking responsibility for learning • Reflecting and evaluating • Conveying ideas in writing (Technology is optional.)	Most SCANS are incorporated into this unit, with an emphasis on: • Monitoring and correcting performance • Sociability • Speaking (Technology is optional.)	ACADEMIC • Discuss learning strategies • Edit a paragraph • Identify parts of a paragraph • Write a paragraph • Plan educational goals	**1:** 0.1.4, 0.2.1, 0.2.2, 0.2.4, 7.1.1, 7.2.1 **2:** 0.1.2, 4.8.1, 6.1.1, 6.7.2, 7.4.1, 7.4.9 **3:** 7.1.1 **4:** 7.2.4, 7.4.1, 7.4.3, 7.4.5
Most EFF skills are incorporated into this unit, with an emphasis on: • Taking responsibility for learning • Reflecting and evaluating • Solving problems and making decisions • Planning (Technology is optional.)	Most SCANS are incorporated into this unit, with an emphasis on: • Responsibility • Self-Management • Decision making • Problem solving • Seeing things in the mind's eye (Technology is optional.)	ACADEMIC • Use context to work out meaning of new words • Create a goal chart and estimate time needed for different goals • Write a paragraph • Identify main ideas in an article • Make vocabulary cards MATH • Create a cluster diagram	**1:** 0.2.4 **2:** 7.1.1, 7.1.2, 7.1.3, 7.1.4, 7.2.4 **3:** 7.2.7, 7.3.2 **4:** 7.2.5, 7.2.7 **5:** 7.2.1, 7.2.2 **6:** 7.2.6 **7:** 7.1.2, 7.2.1, 7.2.4 **R:** 7.1.4, 7.2.1, 7.4.1, 7.4.2 **TP:** 4.8.1, 4.8.5, 4.8.6
Most EFF skills are incorporated into this unit, with an emphasis on: • Learning through research • Using mathematics in problem solving and communication • Planning (Technology is optional.)	Most SCANS are incorporated into this unit, with an emphasis on: • Allocating money • Understanding systems • Acquiring and evaluating information • Decision making (Technology is optional.)	ACADEMIC • Understand main ideas in an article • Organize information in a chart • Write a business letter MATH • Use addition and subtraction to calculate monthly budgeted and actual expenses • Make a budget • Compare prices, fees, and other numerical data	**1:** 1.5.1, 6.1.1, 6.1.2 **2:** 1.2.5 **3:** 7.2.2, 7.2.7 **4:** 1.2.5, 1.3.1, 1.3.2, 1.3.3 **5:** 1.3.1, 1.4.6, 1.5.2 **6:** 1.2.1, 1.2.2 **7:** 1.6.3 **R:** 7.1.4, 7.2.1, 7.4.1, 7.4.2 **TP:** 1.5.2, 4.8.1, 4.8.5, 4.8.6
Most EFF skills are incorporated into this unit, with an emphasis on: • Learning through research • Listening actively • Reading with understanding • Solving problems and making decisions • Planning (Technology is optional.)	Most SCANS are incorporated into this unit, with an emphasis on: • Self-management • Acquiring and evaluating information • Decision making • Writing • Reasoning (Technology is optional.)	ACADEMIC • Make inferences from reading a text • Understand steps in a process • Make notes and use them to write a formal letter MATH • Interpret a bar chart • Create a bar chart • Compare numerical and other data	**1:** 1.4.1, 1.4.2 **2:** 1.4.2 **3:** 1.4.2 **4:** 7.2.4 **5:** 7.2.6, 7.2.7 **6:** 6.7.2 **7:** 1.4.6 **R:** 7.1.4, 7.2.1, 7.4.1, 7.4.2 **TP:** 4.8.1, 4.8.5, 4.8.6
Most EFF skills are incorporated into this unit, with an emphasis on: • Learning through research • Speaking so others can understand • Listening actively • Guiding others • Cooperating with others (Technology is optional.)	Most SCANS are incorporated into this unit, with an emphasis on: • Sociability • Teaching others • Exercising leadership • Interpreting and communicating information • Listening • Speaking • Decision making (Technology is optional.)	ACADEMIC • Make inferences from reading a text MATH • Measure distances on a map and use a scale to calculate real distances • Use addition and multiplication to calculate journey times by road	**1:** 2.1.1 **2:** 0.1.2 **3:** 2.5.4, 2.5.5 **4:** 2.5.4, 2.5.6 **5:** 1.9.1, 1.9.3, 1.9.4 **6:** 2.1.1, 7.5.1 **7:** 2.1.1, 2.6.1 **R:** 7.1.4, 7.2.1, 7.4.1, 7.4.2 **TP:** 4.8.1, 4.8.5, 4.8.6

CASAS: Numbers in bold indicate lesson numbers; **R** indicates review lesson; **TP** indicates team project.

CONTENTS

Theme	Unit and page number	Life Skills	Language Functions	Grammar	Vocabulary
Health	**5 Health** *Page 81*	• Fill out a health insurance form • Interpret nutrition labels • Interpret medicine labels	• Talk about good and bad health habits • Describe symptoms of illnesses • Talk about health advice • Compare types of health insurance	• The present perfect continuous—affirmative, negative, and question forms • Indirect speech—report statements using *tell* and *say*	• Health insurance: *dental coverage, dependent, provider, prescription* • Nutrition: *calories, carbohydrates, cholesterol, fat, fiber, protein, sodium, vitamins* • Types of medicines: *antibiotic, capsule, drops, insulin, mouthwash*
Occupational knowledge	**6 Getting Hired** *Page 101*	• Complete a skills inventory • Conduct a job search • Write a resume • Write a cover letter • Prepare for a job interview	• Ask questions to facilitate a job search • Describe past employment experience	• Adjective clauses—restrictive and non-restrictive • The past perfect	• Job skills: *efficient, responsible, detail-oriented, team player* • Job titles: *accountant, assembler, lawyer, receptionist* • Job application materials: *certificate, resume, transcript, letter of recommendation*
Occupational knowledge	**7 On the Job** *Page 121*	• Communicate problems to a supervisor • Write a letter asking for a raise • Make ethical decisions	• Discuss appropriate workplace behavior • Get someone's attention politely • Check that you have understood • Suggest a solution • Discuss workplace ethics	• The passive voice • Tag questions	• Jobs: *benefits, career opportunities, grooming, human resources, job evaluation, raise*
Government and law	**8 Civic Responsibility** *Page 141*	• Understand civic responsibility • Apply for a driver's license • Respond to a jury summons • Fill out tax forms	• Discuss community responsibilities • Discuss community problems • Express opinions	• Passive modals	• Civic responsibilities: *jury summons, parking ticket, income tax, car registration, judge, jury, trial* • Tax forms: *exemption, owe, refund, withhold, file, spouse, joint return* • The electoral process: *elected, step down, term, ballot, campaign, nomination, vote*

Vocabulary List *Pages 161–163*
Grammar Reference *Pages 164–165*
Listening Scripts *Pages 166–169*
Skills Index *Pages 170–171*
Map of the United States *Page 172*

EFF	SCANS (Workplace)	Academic/Math	CASAS
Most EFF skills are incorporated into this unit, with an emphasis on: • Learning through research • Reading with understanding • Using mathematics in problem solving and communication • Advocating and influencing (Technology is optional.)	Most SCANS are incorporated into this unit, with an emphasis on: • Understanding systems • Acquiring and evaluating information • Interpreting and communicating information • Reading • Decision making • Reasoning (Technology is optional.)	ACADEMIC • Read for detail • Identify main ideas of a paragraph • Write a summary MATH • Interpret a bar graph • Create a bar graph • Calculate percentages • Interpret amounts in grams and percentages on a food label	**1:** 3.5.8, 3.5.9, 6.4.3, 6.7.2 **2:** 3.1.1 **3:** 3.1.1 **4:** 3.2.3 **5:** 3.5.1 **6:** 3.3.1, 3.3.2, 3.3.3 **7:** 7.2.1, 7.4.2 **R:** 7.1.4, 7.2.1, 7.4.1, 7.4.2 **TP:** 4.8.1, 4.8.5, 4.8.6
Most EFF skills are incorporated into this unit, with an emphasis on: • Taking responsibility for learning • Conveying ideas in writing • Speaking so others can understand • Observing critically • Planning • Cooperating with others (Technology is optional.)	Most SCANS are incorporated into this unit, with an emphasis on: • Responsibility • Self-esteem • Organizing and maintaining information • Writing • Speaking • Reasoning (Technology is optional.)	ACADEMIC • Discuss research strategies • Write a formal letter • Set goals based on self-evaluation MATH • Organize information in chronological order • Rank skills on a numerical scale	**1:** 4.1.9, 4.4.2 **2:** 4.1.8 **3:** 4.1.3 **4:** 4.6.5 **5:** 4.1.2 **6:** 4.1.2 **7:** 4.1.5, 4.1.7 **R:** 7.1.4, 7.2.1, 7.4.1, 7.4.2 **TP:** 4.8.1, 4.8.5, 4.8.6
Most EFF skills are incorporated into this unit, with an emphasis on: • Speaking so others can understand • Listening actively • Observing critically • Solving problems and making decisions • Resolving conflict and negotiating • Cooperating with others (Technology is optional.)	Most SCANS are incorporated into this unit, with an emphasis on: • Monitoring and correcting performance • Responsibility • Self-management • Integrity/honesty • Participating as a member of a team • Listening • Speaking • Problem solving (Technology is optional.)	ACADEMIC • Work out meanings from context • Use critical thinking to analyze problems and solve them MATH • Create a Venn diagram • Interpret a flow chart	**1:** 4.4.1 **2:** 0.1.2, 0.1.6 **3:** 4.4.1, 4.8.1, 4.8.5, 7.3.2, 7.4.8 **4:** 0.1.2, 0.1.6 **5:** 4.8.1, 4.8.5, 4.8.6, 7.2.2, 7.2.5, 7.2.7, 7.3.2, 7.3.4 **6:** 4.1.6, 4.4.2, 7.2.1, 7.2.4 **7:** 4.4.1, 4.4.2 **R:** 7.1.4, 7.2.1, 7.4.1, 7.4.2 **TP:** 4.8.1, 4.8.5, 4.8.6
Most EFF skills are incorporated into this unit, with an emphasis on: • Taking responsibility for learning • Learning through research • Solving problems and making decisions (Technology is optional.)	Most SCANS are incorporated into this unit, with an emphasis on: • Understanding systems • Responsibility • Self-esteem • Exercising leadership • Listening • Speaking • Problem solving • Seeing things in the mind's eye (Technology is optional.)	ACADEMIC • Use transition words in writing • Write a paragraph describing a process • Understand a speech • Write a speech MATH • Interpret a flow chart • Interpret numerical information • Calculate taxes and tax exemptions	**1:** 5.6.3 **2:** 1.9.2 **3:** 5.3.3, 5.6.3 **4:** 5.4.1, 5.4.3 **5:** 5.1.4 **6:** 5.6.1 **7:** 5.1.4, 5.1.6 **R:** 7.1.4, 7.2.1, 7.4.1, 7.4.2 **TP:** 4.8.1, 4.8.5, 4.8.6

CASAS: Numbers in bold indicate lesson numbers; **R** indicates review lesson; **TP** indicates team project.

Guide to Stand Out

Meeting the Standards has never been easier!

Stand Out is an easy-to-use, standards-based series for adult students that teaches the English skills necessary to be a successful worker, parent, and citizen.

- **Goals:** A roadmap of learning is provided for the student.

- **Life Skills:** State and federally-required life skills and competencies (i.e. EFF, CASAS, SCANS, model standards, etc.) help students meet necessary benchmarks. This unit includes discussion of civics, citizenship, and community issues.

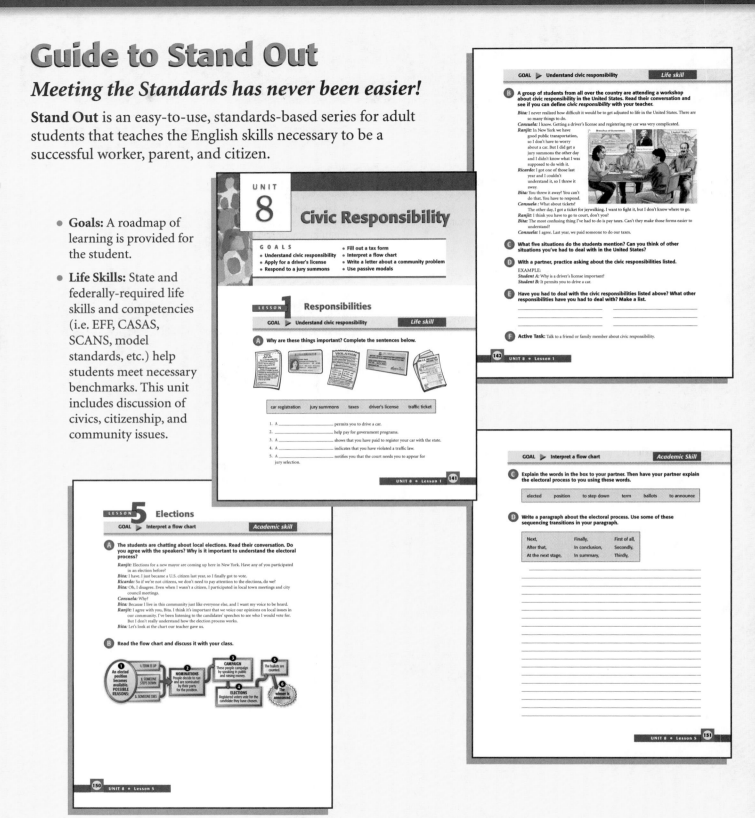

- **Academic Skills:** Students develop higher level skills to insure continued academic success. In this case, an emphasis is placed on interpreting a flow chart, explaining a process, and utilizing sequencing transitions.

Grammar: Charts clearly explain grammar points, and are followed by controlled exercises leading into open-ended ones.

GOAL ▶ Use passive modals   *Grammar*

E Study the chart below with your teacher.

Passive modals				
Passive subject	Modal	be	Past participle	Example sentence
Schools	should	be	built	More schools should be built.
Taxes	need to	be	increased	Taxes need to be increased.
Children	must	be	protected	Children must be protected.
Parents	have to	be	involved	Parents have to be involved.

F Think of three problems you would like to solve in your community. Write three sentences using passive modals.

1. _____
2. _____
3. _____

G Kwan's election speech has three parts. Look for each part in her speech on page 155.

Introduction	She introduces herself and explains why she is running for office.
Body	She tells her audience what she plans to do if she is elected.
Conclusion	She reminds her audience to vote and tells them once again what changes she will make to the community.

H Imagine you are running for mayor of your community. How would you introduce yourself? What problems would you like to solve? On a separate sheet of paper, write a speech that you would give if you were running for mayor. Practice it and give your speech to the class.

I Active Task: Look in the newspaper or on the Internet to find who is mayor or who is running for mayor in your town or city. What issues are they concerned about? What problems do they want to solve?

156 UNIT 8 ● Lesson 7

Review

A Recall what you learned about each of the following topics. Without looking back in the book, what is the most important thing you learned about each?

Topic	The most important thing I learned
A jury summons	
A driver's license	
Income tax	
Community problems	
The electoral process	

B Are the following statements true or false?

○ True ○ False   You have to be 18 to apply for a driver's license.
○ True ○ False   You must reply to a jury summons.
○ True ○ False   You have to be a U.S. citizen to serve on a jury.
○ True ○ False   Everyone must file his or her income tax return separately.
○ True ○ False   If you pay too much tax, the government will give you a refund.
○ True ○ False   Only U.S. citizens can get involved in the community.

C What are three problems in your community you'd like to solve? How would you solve them?

Problem	Solution
1.	
2.	
3.	

UNIT 8 ● Review 157

Review: A summary of key grammar, vocabulary, academic skills, and life skills gives students an opportunity to synthesize what they have learned.

T E A M PROJECT

Conduct an election

With a team, you will prepare a candidate for an election. As a class, you will conduct an election.

1. Form a campaign committee with four or five students. Choose positions for each member of your team.

Position	Job Description	Student Name
Student 1 Leader	See that everyone speaks English. See that everyone participates.	
Student 2 Secretary	Take notes and write candidate's speech.	
Student 3 Presidential candidate	Give speech to class.	
Students 4/5 Member (s)	Help secretary and candidate with their work.	

2. With your team, decide who will be running for class president. Announce the nomination to the class.
3. Members: Create a ballot with all the nominees' names on it. Make a ballot box for students to put their ballots in after they vote.
4. Decide what issues are most important and write a campaign speech.
5. Candidates give speeches to the class.
6. Vote.
7. Count the ballots and announce the winner.

UNIT 8 ● Team Project 159

Team Projects: Project-based activities utilize SCANS competencies (e.g., making decisions, working on a team, developing interpersonal skills, etc.) and provide motivation for students.

PRONUNCIATION

Intonation. We use a falling-rising intonation ⤴ when information is less important, and a falling intonation ⤵ when it is more important. Listen to each sentence below and mark the intonation of each clause with an arrow. Add your own example for number 4.

1. I don't believe in the death penalty, but I think violent criminals should be punished.
2. If more training were available, there wouldn't be so many unemployed people.
3. If people don't vote, they shouldn't complain about who gets elected.
4. _____

LEARNER LOG

In this unit, you learned many things about civic responsibility. How comfortable do you feel doing each of the skills listed below? Rate your comfort level on a scale of 1 to 4.
1 = Not so comfortable 2 = Need more practice 3 = Comfortable 4 = Very comfortable
If you circle 1 or 2, write down the page number where you can review this skill.

Life Skill	Comfort Level	Page(s)
I can apply for a driver's license.	1 2 3 4	____
I can respond to a jury summons.	1 2 3 4	____
I can fill out a tax form.	1 2 3 4	____
I can identify community problems and possible solutions.	1 2 3 4	____
I can write a letter to a local official about a community problem.	1 2 3 4	____
I can communicate opinions about community issues.	1 2 3 4	____

Grammar		
I can use noun clauses.	1 2 3 4	____
I can use passives with modals.	1 2 3 4	____

Academic		
I can interpret a flow chart about the electoral process.	1 2 3 4	____
I can explain the electoral process.	1 2 3 4	____
I can understand key points of a speech.	1 2 3 4	____
I can write a speech.	1 2 3 4	____

Reflection
Wow! You've finished Stand Out! You should be very proud of yourself. Remember, your learning doesn't stop just because you've finished this book. Learning is something that will continue for the rest of your life. And the skills that you've learned in this course will help you Stand Out in everything you do. Good luck!

160 UNIT 8 ● Pronunciation and Learner Log

Pronunciation: Specific pronunciation problems are targeted and corrected.

Learner Log: The final section of each unit provides opportunity for learner self-assessment.

LESSON PLAN • Unit 8: Civic Responsibility   LESSON 1 • Responsibilities

> **LESSON PLAN**
>
> *Objectives:*
> Understand civic responsibility and
> interpret official forms
> *Key vocabulary:*
> civic responsibility, registration, ticket,
> jaywalking, public transportation, jury
> summons, notify

TB Pre-Assessment: Use the *Stand Out*
ExamView® Pro *Test Bank* for Unit 8.
(optional)

Warm-up and Review: 5–10 min. `1.5+`

Ask students to recall what they studied in the
workplace units. Have them make a list of the
most important things they learned. Review
their points that are related to workplace
responsibility.

Introduction: 10–15 min. `1.5+`

Ask students the following questions and ask for
a show of hands:
How many of you drive a car?
How many of you have a driver's license?
How many of you vote?
How many of you pay taxes?

State the Objectives: *Today you will define civic*
responsibility and identify the responsibilities
you have here in the United States. In the rest of
the unit, you will learn how to handle those
responsibilities.

Presentation 1: 10–15 min. `1.5+`

A **Why are these things important?**
Complete the sentences below.

Have students use the words from the vocabulary
box to name the documents pictured. Complete
this vocabulary exercise as a class. Some students
may want to discuss personal experiences dealing
with these civic forms. Allow only one example for
each form as students will have a chance to share
experiences later in the lesson.

Pronunciation: An optional
pronunciation activity is found on the
final page of this unit. This pronunciation
activity may be introduced during any lesson in
this unit, especially if students need practice with
rising and falling intonation to indicate degree of
importance in information. (See pages 160 and
160a for Unit 8 Pronunciation.)

STANDARDS CORRELATIONS

CASAS: 5.6.3
SCANS: **Interpersonal** Participates as a Member of a
Team, Works with Diversity
Information Acquires and Evaluates Information,
Organizes and Maintains Information, Interprets and
Communicates Information
Basic Skills Reading, Writing, Listening, Speaking
Thinking Skills Creative Thinking, Reasoning

Personal Qualities Responsibility, Sociability, Self-
Management
EFF: **Communication** Read with Understanding, Convey
Ideas in Writing, Speak So Others Can Understand, Listen
Actively
Decision Making Plan
Interpersonal Cooperate with Others

141a LP UNIT 8 ● Lesson 1

- **Lesson Plan:** A
  complete lesson plan
  for each page in the
  student book is
  provided using
  nationally-accepted
  curriculum design.

- **Pacing Guidelines:**
  Class-length icons offer
  three different pacing
  strategies.

- **CD Icon:** Supplemental
  activities found on the
  Activity Bank CD-ROM
  are noted with an icon.

- Supplemental warm-up
  activities prepare
  students for lessons.

- Suggested Internet
  activities expose
  students to technology
  and real world
  activities.

Civic Responsibility

A. Create a matching activity by writing definitions in your own words for each of the words in the first column. Write the definitions in the second column, but don't write them directly across from the words. (Mix them up.)

1. car registration	
2. driver's license	
3. jury summons	
4. taxes	
5. traffic ticket	
6. voter registration	

B. Now give your paper to a partner and see if he or she can complete the matching activity by drawing lines from the words to the definitions.

C. Answer the following questions about yourself. Then interview your partner with the same questions. Put a check in the correct column.

	YOU		YOUR PARTNER	
	YES	NO	YES	NO
1. Do you drive a car? If yes, is your car registered?				
2. Do you have a driver's license?				
3. Have you ever received a jury summons? If yes, did you fill it out and send it back?				
4. Have you ever gotten a traffic ticket?				
5. Do you pay taxes?				
6. Are you registered to vote?				

D. Compare your experiences with your partner.

Heinle & Heinle © 2002
Stand Out 4 Activity Bank

Civic Responsibility

CHALLENGE 1 ► *Supposed to, required to, allowed to*

Example	Explanation
You are **supposed to** return the jury summons. You are **not supposed to** tear up the form.	**(Not) supposed to** is a reminder of a legal obligation or a rule.
You are **required to** have a driver's license to drive. You are **not required to** be an organ donor.	**Required to** shows legal obligation. **Not required to** shows no legal obligation.
You are **allowed/permitted to** smoke outside. You are **not allowed/permitted to** smoke inside.	**Allowed/permitted to** shows permission. **Not allowed/permitted to** shows something is against the rules.

• The verb **be** is used with **supposed to, required to,** and **allowed to.**
• Use the base form of a verb after **supposed to, required to,** and **allowed to.**

A Write *a, b, c,* or *d* to show how the underlined expression is used.

a. legal obligation or a rule   b. no legal obligation   c. permission   d. against the rules

EXAMPLE: _d_ Non-citizens are <u>not allowed to</u> vote.

1. ____ Citizens are <u>not required to</u> vote.
2. ____ Non-citizens are <u>permitted to</u> attend local town meetings.
3. ____ Anyone is <u>allowed to</u> voice his or her opinion at these meetings.
4. ____ Non-citizens are <u>not permitted to</u> run for public office.
5. ____ Everyone is <u>supposed to</u> file an income tax return.
6. ____ You're not <u>supposed to</u> throw it away.
7. ____ You are <u>required to</u> report interest from savings on your return.
8. ____ If you're married, you are <u>allowed to</u> file a joint return or a separate return.

B Answer each question using the words in parenthese s.

EXAMPLE: Can I get a driver's license? (yes / be allowed to)
   Yes, you are allowed to get a driver's license.

1. Can I drive a car without a license? (no / not / be permitted to)

2. Do I have to take a written test? (yes / be supposed to)

3. Do I have to study the driver's handbook first? (no / not / be required to)

4. Do I have to fill out an application for the road test? (yes / be required to)

5. Can I smoke during the road test? (no / not be supposed)

6. Can I drive if my license is suspended? (no / not / be allowed to)

Supposed to, required to, allowed to

Pre-Test Unit 8: Civic Responsibility

A. Choose the best answer.

____ 1. A _____ proves that you are legally allowed to operate an automobile.
   a. traffic ticket   c. car registration
   b. driver's license application   d. driver's license

____ 2. You must pay _____ taxes to the government if you work.
   a. income   c. business
   b. property   d. sales

____ 3. A _____ is sent to you when the court needs your services.
   a. lawsuit   c. tax form
   b. jury summons   d. voter registration

____ 4. If you receive a _____, you have done something against the law.
   a. car registration   c. jury summons
   b. traffic ticket   d. tax form

____ 5. What is the correct order of the electoral process?
   a. campaign, nominations, position becomes available, elections
   b. position becomes available, campaign, nominations, elections
   c. nominations, position becomes available, campaign, elections
   d. position becomes available, nominations, campaign, elections

B. Write one solution for each problem below.

6. overcrowded freeways
_____

7. dangerous crosswalks
_____

8. gangs in a residential neighborhood
_____

- **Activity Bank CD-ROM:** Hours of motivating and creative reinforcement activities are provided to follow student book lessons. Instructors can download activities and add or adapt them to student needs. The audio component for listening activities will also be on CD-ROMs. Cassettes are available for instructors who prefer them.

- ***Stand Out Grammar Challenge:*** Optional workbook activities provide supplemental exercises for students who desire even more contextual grammar and vocabulary practice.

- ***Stand Out ExamView®Pro Test Bank:*** Innovative test bank CD-ROM allows for pre-and post-unit quizzes. Teachers can easily print out predetermined tests, or modify them to create their own customized (including computer-based) assessments.

Getting to Know You

GOALS

- Fill out an admission application
- Discuss learning strategies
- Edit a paragraph
- Recognize word families

College admission application

GOAL ▶ Fill out an admission application *Life skill*

A Imagine that you have decided to take some classes at a college. Fill out the section of the admission application below.

CCC   **CANYON COUNTY COLLEGE**   **CCC**
              Admission Application

1. _____   _____   _____
         Last Name   First Name   Middle Name

2. Date of Birth ___/___/___   3. (___)-___-_____   4. ___ **XXX-XX-XXXX** ___
         Mo Day Year   Area Code Telephone Number   Student ID Number

5. Sex: Male   6. Place of Birth _____   _____
         Female   City   State or Foreign Country

7. Citizen of what country _____

8. What is the highest level of education you have achieved? _____
_____

9. What is your educational goal? _____

B Talk to three students. Find out their first names, where they are from, and one other piece of interesting information (tidbit) about them. Then introduce your new friends to another group of students.

GOAL ▶ **Discuss learning strategies**

Academic skill

A Learning a new language takes place inside and outside the classroom. Below is a list of some strategies you can use to learn a new language. Read them with your teacher.

Learning Strategies

Learn grammar rules

Listen to the radio in English

Read English language books, magazines, and newspapers

Talk to native speakers

Watch TV in English

Write in English

B Think of some other strategies that are not listed above and add them to the list.

C Answer the following questions about your personal studying strategies.

1. Where do you usually study? _____

2. What strategies do you use inside the classroom? _____
   _____

3. What strategies do you use outside the classroom? _____
   _____

4. Choose two strategies that you don't use now, but that you would like to use in the future. _____
   _____

D Share your answers with another student.

LESSON 3 **Checking your work**

GOAL ▶ **Edit a paragraph**   *Academic skill*

A Look at the first draft of Takuji's paragraph. There are eight more errors. Can you find and correct them?

> ### My Goals
>
>   Ever since I came to the United State^s, I have had three goal. First I
>
> need to improve my English by going at school every day and studying at
>
> night. Once my English are better, I will look for a job that pays more
>
> money. Finally, when I have saved up enough money. I will buy a house new
>
> for my family. This are the three goals that I made when I first come to the
>
> united states.

B Write each of the errors in the chart below. Write the correct form and identify the type of error using the words in the box.

punctuation	capitalization	spelling	word order
singular/plural	verb tense	word choice	subject/verb agreement

Error	Correction	Type of error

C **What is a paragraph? Discuss the words in italics with your teacher.**

A paragraph is a group of sentences (usually 5–7 sentences) about the *same topic*. A *topic sentence* is usually the first sentence. It introduces the *topic* or *main idea. Support sentences* are the sentences that follow the topic sentence. They give *details* about the topic. A *conclusion sentence* is the last sentence of the paragraph and it summarizes what has been written.

D **Look at Takuji's final version of his paragraph. Can you find each of the sentence types?**

My Goals
Ever since I came to the United States, I have had three goals. First, I need to improve my English by going to school every day and studying at night. Once my English is better, I will look for a job that pays more money. Finally, when I have saved up enough money, I will buy a new house for my family. These are the three goals that I made when I first came to the United States.

E **What are your goals? On a separate sheet of paper, write a paragraph about your goals. Make sure your first sentence is a topic sentence. Follow your topic sentence with support sentences and finish with a conclusion sentence.**

F **Exchange paragraphs with a partner. Check your partner's work for errors using the error types on the previous page.**

LESSON 4 Word families

| GOAL ▶ Recognize word families | *Academic skill* |

A In this book, you will be learning many new strategies to help you learn and remember vocabulary. The first strategy involves word families. What do you think a word family is? Look at the example below.

Noun	Verb	Adjective	Adverb
creation	create	creative	creatively

B Read the following paragraph. There are five words that belong to the same word family. Can you find and underline them?

Learning new vocabulary is very important for second language learners. To be successful, you need to be organized. Good organization requires writing down the new words you learn and finding out their meanings. You should organize the words so you can easily find them. Once you learn how to keep a well-organized vocabulary list, you can say, "I have good organizational skills!"

C Complete the following chart with words in the same word family. You may need to use a dictionary or ask another student for help.

Noun	Verb	Adjective	Adverb
		educational	
success			
	decide		
			actively

Balancing Your Life

GOALS

- Use *used to*
- Create a goal chart
- Discuss obstacles and solutions
- Give and respond to advice

- Use adjective clauses
- Write a paragraph
- Understand time management skills

LESSON 1

Where did you use to study?

GOAL ▶ Use *used to*   *Grammar*

A Bita and Satoru are new students at Bellingham Adult School. Listen to their conversation on the first day of class.

B With a partner, answer the following questions about Bita and Satoru. You may have to guess some of the answers.

1. How old are they?

2. What do they do?

3. Where are they from?

4. Why are they studying English?

Bita   Satoru

C Bita and Satoru both talk about things they did in the past and things they do now. Listen again and make two lists in your notebook.

D Study the chart with your teacher.

Used to	
Example sentence	**Rule**
Satoru *used to* <u>attend</u> this school five years ago. Bita *used to* <u>be</u> an architect in Iran.	Affirmative: *used to* + base verb
Bita *did not use to* <u>go</u> to school at night. Satoru *didn't use to* <u>take</u> care of his grandchildren.	Negative: *did + not (didn't) + use to +* base verb. Incorrect: ~~I didn't used to go to school.~~
Did Satoru *use to* <u>work</u>? *Did* Bita *use to* <u>study</u> English?	Yes/no question: *did + subject + use to +* base verb. Incorrect: ~~Did Bita used to live in Iran?~~
Where *did* Satoru *use to* <u>work</u>? What *did* Bita *use to* <u>study</u>?	*Wh-* question: *wh-* word + *did* + subject + *use to* + base verb
Used to + base verb expresses a past habit or state that is now different.	

E Look at the examples that you wrote in exercise C on the previous page. With a partner, make sentences and questions about what Bita and Satoru *used to* do.

EXAMPLE:
Bita used to go to another school in the daytime.

F Think about things you used to do. Write three sentences below and share them with your class.

1. _____

2. _____

3. _____

G Write three *Wh-* questions using *used to.* Then ask your partner.

EXAMPLE:
Where did you use to work?

1. _____

2. _____

3. _____

H **Complete the following sentences with *used to* or the simple present verb.**

EXAMPLE:
Bita used to live with her family, but now she lives alone.

1. Bita _____ (go) to school in the daytime, but now she

   _____ (go) at night.

2. She _____ (be) an administrative assistant now, but she

   _____ (be) an architect in Iran.

3. Satoru _____ (attend) class during the day, but now he

   _____ (attend) at night.

4. He just _____ (go) to school and _____ (help) his

   grandchildren now, but he _____ (assemble) computers.

I **Look at the pictures below. Write sentences comparing the past to the present.**

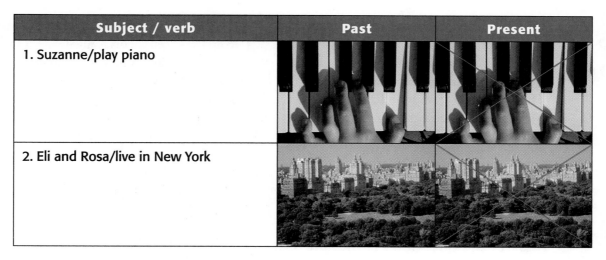

Subject / verb	Past	Present
1. Suzanne/play piano		
2. Eli and Rosa/live in New York		

EXAMPLE:
Bita used to live with her family, but now she doesn't.

1. _____

2. _____

J **Write two sentences comparing your past and present habits.**

1. _____

2. _____

LESSON 2 What are your goals?

GOAL ▶ Create a goal chart   *Academic skill*

A **Read the paragraph about Bita's goals. Use the context (other words around the vocabulary word) to work out the meanings of the words in italics. Do the first one with your teacher.**

My name is Bita and I'm from Iran. I've been in the United States for six years. In my country I was an *architect* and I designed schools and hospitals, but in the United States, I don't have the right *qualifications* to be an architect. I have a plan. I'm going to learn English, go to school for architecture, and become an architect in the United States. Here is my dream. In eight years, I will be an architect working for a *firm* with three other partners. We will design and build homes in *suburban* neighborhoods. I will live in a nice home that I designed and I will look for the man of my dreams to share my life with me. How does that sound to you?

B **Read the paragraph about Satoru. Use the context to work out the meanings of the words in italics.**

I'm Satoru and I've been in the United States since 1975. I came here as an *immigrant* from Japan. I used to work for a computer company, but now I'm *retired*. I help take care of my grandchildren while their parents are working. But I also do something else on the side. I make jewelry to sell to local jewelers. My father was a jeweler in Japan and he taught me his art. My goal is to help send my grandchildren to college, so I've saved every penny I make from the jewelry. This is my dream. In five years, my oldest grandchild will teach elementary school in the community where she lives and she will *raise* her own family. My other grandchild will study medicine at one of the best schools in the country because he wants to be a *surgeon*. I hope that all of their dreams come true.

C **Answer the questions with a partner.**

1. What are Bita's and Satoru's goals?

2. What are they doing to make their goals a reality?

3. What are their dreams?

D **What are some examples of different goals? Discuss your ideas with your teacher.**

E **What are your future goals? Write them down on a separate piece of paper.**

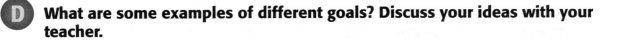

F Listen to the conversation that Bita is having with her friend, Yoshiko, and fill in Bita's goal chart with the missing steps and dates.

Goal: To become an architect and become a partner in a firm	
Steps	Completion Date
Step 1: Study English.	Spring 2004
Step 2:	Fall 2004
Step 3:	
Step 4: Become an intern.	Summer 2008
Step 5:	Winter 2009
Step 6: Become a partner in a firm.	

G Take out the piece of paper where you wrote your goals. Choose one goal and fill in the chart below. Make sure you list all of the steps and completion dates.

Goal:	
Steps	Completion Date
Step 1:	
Step 2:	
Step 3:	
Step 4:	
Step 5:	
Step 6:	

H **Active Task:** Use your goal chart to track your goal. Next to each *Completion Date*, write the actual date that you complete each step.

Obstacles and solutions

GOAL ▷ Discuss obstacles and solutions

A Sometimes, we have problems achieving our goals. These problems are called *obstacles.* In order to overcome these obstacles, it can be a good idea to brainstorm a number of different possible solutions. Look at the example below.

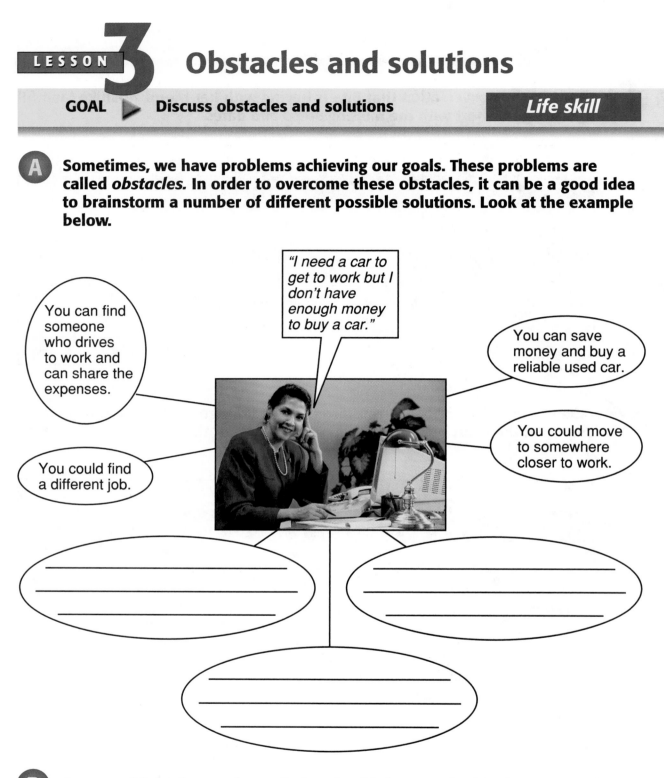

B Can you think of any other solutions? Add them to the blank circles in the cluster diagram above.

C **Read each of the situations below and try to come up with two possible solutions for each. Use *can* or *could* when writing your solutions.**

1. Magda wants to go back to school but she has two children that she has to take care of. One of her children is in fourth grade and goes to school from 7:30 A.M.–2 P.M., but her other child is a toddler who isn't in school yet.

   EXAMPLE: Solution 1: ***She could ask a family member to take care of her toddler so she can go to school during the day.***

   Solution 2: _____

   _____

   Solution 3: _____

   _____

2. Frank wants to open up a restaurant in his neighborhood. He can get a loan to buy the property, but he won't have enough money to pay his employees until the restaurant starts making money.

   Solution 1: _____

   _____

   Solution 2: _____

   _____

   Solution 3: _____

   _____

3. Sergei works for a computer software company and wants to move up to be a project manager. The problem is he needs to get more training before he can move up, but he doesn't have time to do training during the day.

   Solution 1: _____

   _____

   Solution 2: _____

   _____

   Solution 3: _____

   _____

D **Now take one of your goals that you wrote for exercise E on page 4 and think of an obstacle that might get in your way. Make a cluster diagram like the one on page 6 and brainstorm different solutions with a partner.**

What should I do?

| GOAL ▶ Give and respond to advice | Life skill |

A Read the following ways of giving and responding to advice.

Problem	Give advice
Magda wants to go back to school but she has two children that she has to take care of. One of them is a toddler who isn't in school yet.	*Why don't you* ask your mother to take care of him?
	How about going to night school?
	You should take some courses at home on the Internet.
	You could find a school with a daycare facility.

Respond to advice (positive)	Respond to advice (negative)
That's a great idea.	I don't think I can do that because . . .
Why didn't I think of that?	That doesn't sound possible because . . .
That's what I'll do.	That won't work because . . .

B Look back at the problems on page 7. Imagine that you have these problems. With a partner, make conversations like the one below. Use different ways of giving and responding to advice from the chart above.

EXAMPLE:
Student A: I want to go back to school, but I have a young child to take care of.
Student B: Why don't you ask your mother to take care of him?
Student A: That won't work because she lives too far away.
Student B: Then how about taking some courses on the Internet?
Student A: That's a great idea!

C Listen to the following people talking to their friends about their problems. After you listen to each conversation, write the problem and two pieces of advice that each person receives.

Miyuki	Problem	Advice 1	Advice 2
Ron			
Patty			

D **Active Task:** Where can you go to get advice if you have a problem? Make a list of agencies or centers that can offer advice or counseling for different types of problems. Go to the public library or look up counseling agencies on the Internet to find more information.

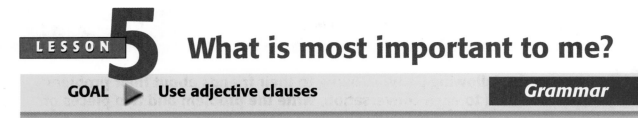

What is most important to me?

GOAL ▶ **Use adjective clauses** *Grammar*

A **Look at the pictures and listen to Eliana talking about what is important to her. Then read the paragraphs below.**

This is a picture of the house where I grew up in Argentina. It's very important to me because it holds a lot of memories. This is the garden where I played with my brothers and sisters, and the veranda where I often sat with my parents in the evenings, listening to their stories and watching the stars and dreaming about my future.

This is the person who influenced me the most when I was young. She was my teacher in first grade, and we stayed friends until I left home. She was always so calm and gave me good advice. She was the kind of person who is able to give you another perspective on a problem and makes you feel hopeful, no matter how troubled you are.

This is my daily journal. I use it to write about my feelings and hopes and it helps me to understand them better. Sometimes I just write about things that happened to me during the day. My journal is something which helps me to focus on the important things in my life.

B **Read the paragraphs again and underline the words *who, which, that,* and *where.***

C **Choose the correct answer below.**

1. We use *which* or *that* for ○ places ○ people ○ things.

2. We use *who* for ○ places ○ people ○ things.

3. We use *where* for ○ places ○ people ○ things.

Study the chart with your teacher.

Adjective clauses		
Main clause	**Relative pronoun**	**Adjective clause**
This is the place	*where*	I grew up.
She is the person	*who*	influenced me the most.
A journal is something	*that (which)*	can help you focus on important things.
Adjective clauses describe a preceding noun.		

E **Combine the following sentences using adjective clauses.**

EXAMPLE: This is the house. I grew up there. ***This is the house where I grew up.***

1. That is the city. I was born there.

_____

2. I have a friend. She helps me when I am sick.

_____

3. Do you know a school? I can learn about computers.

_____

4. She has many problems. They are making her sad.

_____

5. This is a good dictionary. It can help you improve your vocabulary.

_____

6. My son has a new teacher. He gives him a lot of homework.

_____

7. We have some neighbors. They are very friendly.

_____

8. This is a gold ring. It reminds me of my mother.

_____

Look at the pictures below and make sentences about them using adjective clauses.

This is a place where _____.

This is a person who _____.

This is a thing that _____.

 Work in pairs. Make sentences about these nouns using adjective clauses (but don't say the noun in your sentence). Your partner will guess which place, person, or thing you are talking about.

EXAMPLE:
Student A: It's a thing that opens doors.
Student B: A key.

Places	People	Things
supermarket	firefighter	key
library	senator	paintbrush
hospital	counselor	diary
hotel	friend	stamp
airport	guide	newspaper
school	lawyer	car

 Choose a place, a person, and a thing. Tell your partner why they are important to you. On a separate sheet of paper, write a description for each one. Use adjective clauses in your description.

LESSON 6 — My favorite person

| GOAL ▶ Write a paragraph | *Academic skill* |

A **Bita wrote a paragraph about her brother. Read the paragraph, then discuss the questions below with your partner.**

Someone Who Has Influenced Me

    The person who has influenced me the most in my life is my brother, Karim. I admire my brother for three reasons. First, he has patience and determination. Second, he does a fantastic job helping the community. Third, he is the type of person who always has time for his friends and family, no matter how busy he is. He has had a very positive influence on my life.

1. What type of person is Bita's brother?

2. Why does Bita admire him?

3. How has he influenced Bita?

B **Now it's your turn to write about a person who has influenced you. Complete the following pre-writing activities before you begin writing.**

- *Brainstorm* (Think about your ideas before you write.)

  Who has influenced you the most in your life? _____

  Why is this person so important to you? List three reasons.

  1. _____

  2. _____

  3. _____

- *Introduce* (Tell your readers what you are writing about.) Write your topic sentence(s) below.

  _____

- *Conclude* (Remind your reader of the main idea but don't restate your topic sentence.) Write your conclusion sentence below.

  _____

C Write a paragraph about the most important person in your life. Start with your topic sentence, put your reasons (support sentences) in the middle, and finish with your conclusion sentence. Remember to write a title.

_____

_____

_____

_____

_____

_____

_____

_____

D Remember the editing techniques you learned in the pre-unit? Reread your paragraph and make any necessary corrections.

E Now share your paragraph with two other students and have them use the questions below to make suggestions for you.

Content	Punctuation and grammar
1. Is there a clear topic sentence that states the main idea? 2. Are there three support sentences that support the main idea? 3. Are the three ideas connected using *first, second,* and *third*? 4. Is there a conclusion sentence that restates the main idea in different words?	1. Is the beginning of every sentence capitalized? 2. Is every sentence punctuated correctly? 3. Are all the words spelled correctly? 4. Do the subjects agree with the verbs? 5. Are the verb forms correct? 6. Are the verb tenses correct?

F Take out a clean sheet of paper and rewrite your paragraph.

G **Active Task:** Read your paragraph to the person you wrote about or to someone who knows that person.

Time management

GOAL ▶ Understand time management skills   *Academic skill*

A **Are you an organized person? Do you . . .**

❑ try to do everything but run out of time?

❑ always plan everything far in advance?

❑ dislike planning things too far ahead?

❑ tend to leave things to the last minute?

❑ get upset by last-minute changes to your schedule?

❑ only plan for important tasks like exams and job interviews?

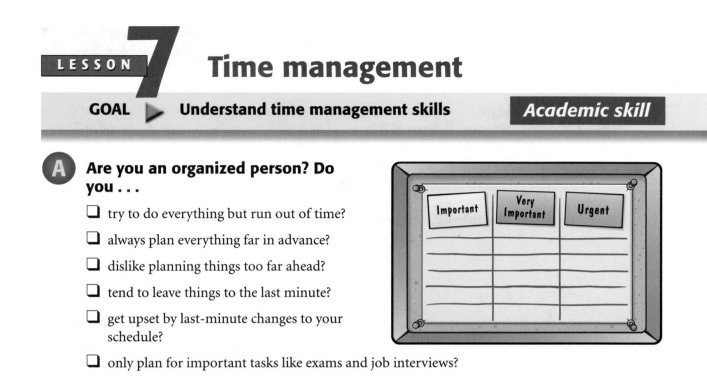

B **What do you know about time management strategies? Make a list of any time management strategies that you use.**

_____   _____

_____   _____

_____   _____

C **Read the following paragraphs about time management. Write the number of each paragraph next to the correct topic below.**

_____ How can I use my time more efficiently?

_____ Why is good health important to time management?

_____ How can I be organized?

_____ What is time management? Why is it important?

_____ How can I get important tasks done first?

Time Management Skills

(1) Finding enough time to study is very important for all students. There are a number of time management strategies that can help you to manage your time wisely. You can use them to *accomplish* the goals you have set for yourself without *sacrificing* the time you spend with your family and friends.

(2) One of the best ways to stay organized is to keep a schedule. Write down everything you need to do in a week. This includes work, study, children, shopping, and other tasks. Then *allocate* a time slot to each of these tasks. Be *realistic* about the time you will need for each task. Then check off each task when you have completed it.

(3) It is a good idea to *prioritize* your tasks in order of importance. Make a "To Do" list of all your tasks. Divide your list into A, B, and C. The A list is for tasks you need to do today. The B list is for tasks you need to do tomorrow. The C list is for tasks you need to do this month. This will help you to get your most important tasks done first. You can also list tasks according to urgency: tasks you have to do, tasks you should do, and tasks you'd like to do if you have time.

(4) Another time management strategy is to combine two or more tasks and do them *simultaneously*. You can listen to audio study tapes while you are on the bus, for example. Or, you can review verb tenses while you are eating lunch.

(5) Remember that good health is also important for managing your time effectively. If you are burned out or overtired, you cannot do your best. You need to allow time for rest and for exercise. You also need to have time to spend with family, friends, and other people who are important to you. Set realistic *deadlines* and mark them on your schedule. Don't get upset if you cannot accomplish all your goals. Be positive about your *achievements* and reward yourself for the goals that you have accomplished.

D **Use the diagram below to record the main points of the reading.**

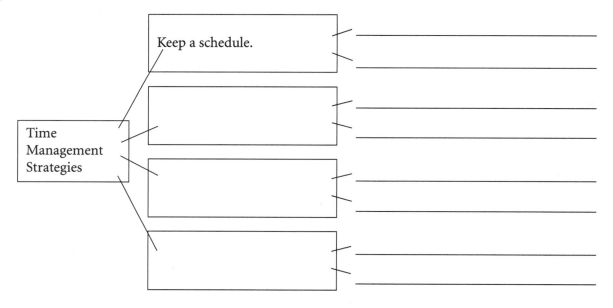

E **Find the following words in the reading and use the context to work out their meaning: *accomplish, sacrificing, allocate, realistic, prioritize, simultaneously, deadlines, achievements.***

F **Active Task:** Go to the library or use the Internet to find tips on time management. Find one tip and tell your classmates.

Review

A) **It is useful to make vocabulary cards to practice new words and phrases. Look at the sample card below.**

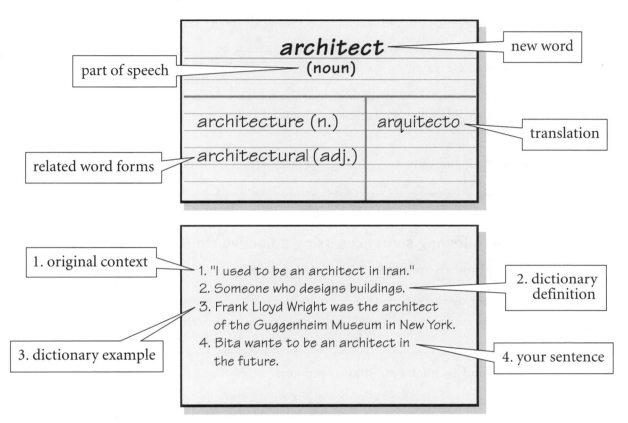

part of speech

architect ← new word
(noun)

| architecture (n.) | arquitecto |
| architectural (adj.) | |

related word forms

translation

1. original context

1. "I used to be an architect in Iran."
2. Someone who designs buildings.
3. Frank Lloyd Wright was the architect of the Guggenheim Museum in New York.
4. Bita wants to be an architect in the future.

3. dictionary example

2. dictionary definition

4. your sentence

 B) **Choose five new words you learned in this unit and make vocabulary cards using note cards. If you don't have cards, use pieces of paper.**

C) **Use the words from this unit to complete these sentences.**

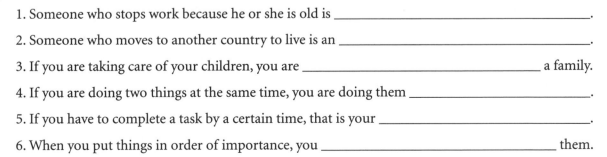

1. Someone who stops work because he or she is old is _____.

2. Someone who moves to another country to live is an _____.

3. If you are taking care of your children, you are _____ a family.

4. If you are doing two things at the same time, you are doing them _____.

5. If you have to complete a task by a certain time, that is your _____.

6. When you put things in order of importance, you _____ them.

Review

D **Make sentences to contrast past and present habits.**

EXAMPLE:

Past: I ate meat.   Present: I don't eat meat now.

I used to eat meat, but now I don't.

1. Past: Paolo didn't have a computer.   Present: He has a computer.

   _____

2. Past: Maria swam every day.   Present: She doesn't swim now.

   _____

3. Past: My children didn't like vegetables.   Present: They like vegetables now.

   _____

4. Past: I didn't study full-time.   Present: Now I study full-time.

   _____

E **Combine the following sentences using adjective clauses.**

1. Esra has many brothers and sisters. They live in Argentina.

   _____

2. This is a good grammar book. It could help you improve your writing.

   _____

3. I am trying to find a school. I can study computers.

   _____

4. E-mail is a type of communication. It is fast and easy to use.

   _____

F **Your friend wants to study at college, but he needs a full-time job at the same time. Make a conversation with your partner. Suggest two or three different solutions to his problem. Use expressions from this unit for giving and responding to advice. Then write the conversation below.**

You: _____

Your friend: _____

You: _____

Your friend: _____

You: _____

Your friend: _____

Create a Goal Chart

With a team, you will create a goal chart for goals you want to accomplish in this class.

1. Form a team with four or five students. Choose positions for each member of your team.

Position	Job Description	Student Name
Student 1 Leader	See that everyone speaks English. See that everyone participates.	
Student 2 Secretary	Take notes and fill out the goal chart.	
Student 3 Designer	Design the goal chart layout.	
Students 4/5 Member(s)	Help the secretary and the designer with their work.	

2. Write down three goals that your team would like to accomplish by the end of this class term. Write down the steps it will take to reach each goal. Write down a completion date for each step.

3. Design a goal chart template. Make sure your chart has room for Steps, Completion Dates, Actual Completion Dates, Obstacles, Solutions, and Time Management Techniques.

4. Write down obstacles that might get in the way of your goals and solutions for each. Add these to your chart.

5. Make a list of five time management techniques that will help you reach your goals and add them to your chart.

PRONUNCIATION

Sentence stress. We can use stress to emphasize words that we want to contrast and to make the meaning clearer. Listen and repeat the first sentence. Then listen to sentences 2, 3, and 4. Underline the stressed words.

1. Last year she studied computers, but this year she wants to study accounting.

2. They used to like skiing, but now they prefer yoga.

3. Cooking is my job, but jewelry-making is my hobby.

4. We weren't able to attend college, so we want our children to graduate.

LEARNER LOG

In this unit, you learned many things about balancing your life. How comfortable do you feel doing each of the skills listed below? Rate your comfort level on a scale of 1 to 4.

1 = Not so comfortable **2** = Need more practice **3** = Comfortable **4** = Very comfortable

If you circle 1 or 2, write down the page number where you can review this skill.

Life Skill	Comfort Level				Page(s)
Identify and discuss future goals.	1	2	3	4	_____
Create a goal chart.	1	2	3	4	_____
Discuss obstacles and solutions.	1	2	3	4	_____
Identify important relationships.	1	2	3	4	_____
Analyze your personal time management techniques.	1	2	3	4	_____

Grammar					
Use *used to* for habits in the past.	1	2	3	4	_____
Contrast past and present habits.	1	2	3	4	_____
Give and respond to advice.	1	2	3	4	_____
Use adjective clauses.	1	2	3	4	_____

Academic Skill					
Use context clues to discover word meaning.	1	2	3	4	_____
Write a paragraph.	1	2	3	4	_____
Read about time management.	1	2	3	4	_____
Analyze a reading on time management.	1	2	3	4	_____

Reflection

Complete the following statements about this unit.

I learned _____

I would like to find out more about _____

I am still confused about _____

Personal Finance

GOALS

- Calculate monthly expenses
- Understand main ideas in a text
- Use contrary-to-fact conditionals
- Interpret credit card information
- Interpret loan information
- Analyze advertising techniques
- Express complaints

LESSON 1

Money in, money out

GOAL ▶ Calculate monthly expenses   *Life skill*

A Think about your personal finances. What do you spend money on every month?

B Listen to Sara and Todd Mason talk about their finances. Fill in the amounts.

Monthly expenses	
Auto	$450
Rent	
Utilities	
Cable/Phone/Internet	
Food	
School supplies	
Clothing	
Medical	
Entertainment	

C Compare your list of categories to the Masons' list. What are the similarities? What are the differences?

D Look at the chart below. The first column, Monthly expenses, lists everything Todd and Sara spend money on. The second column, Budgeted amount, is how much they think they will spend this month. Look at the numbers you wrote on the previous page and transfer them to this column.

E Listen to Sara and Todd talk about what they actually spent in the month of May. Write down their actual expenses in the third column.

Monthly expenses	Budgeted amount	Actual amount spent in May	Difference
Auto	$450	$362.43	
Rent	$1,500	$1,500	$0
Utilities			
Cable/Phone/Internet			
Food			
School			
Clothing			
Medical			
Entertainment			
TOTAL			

F Find the difference between the amount they budgeted and the amount they actually spent and write the amounts in the chart. What is the total amount they budgeted? What is the total amount they spent? What is the difference?

Example:

$212.43
− $200.00
$ 12.43

G **Active Task:** Make a budget like the Masons' budget. Keep track of how much money you spend over the next month. Then adjust your budget if you need to.

LESSON 2 — Savvy Shopper

GOAL ▶ Understand main ideas in a text **Academic skill**

A The Masons have decided to buy a new couch for their family. They want a good-quality piece of furniture that will last a long time. What do you think they will do before buying the couch? Discuss ideas with your teacher.

B Sara did some research on the Internet. Read the web page below to see what information she found.

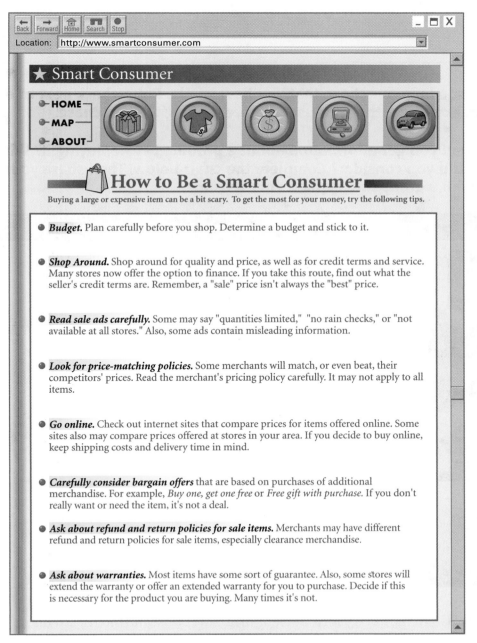

Location: http://www.smartconsumer.com

★ Smart Consumer

- HOME
- MAP
- ABOUT

How to Be a Smart Consumer

Buying a large or expensive item can be a bit scary. To get the most for your money, try the following tips.

- *Budget.* Plan carefully before you shop. Determine a budget and stick to it.

- *Shop Around.* Shop around for quality and price, as well as for credit terms and service. Many stores now offer the option to finance. If you take this route, find out what the seller's credit terms are. Remember, a "sale" price isn't always the "best" price.

- *Read sale ads carefully.* Some may say "quantities limited," "no rain checks," or "not available at all stores." Also, some ads contain misleading information.

- *Look for price-matching policies.* Some merchants will match, or even beat, their competitors' prices. Read the merchant's pricing policy carefully. It may not apply to all items.

- *Go online.* Check out internet sites that compare prices for items offered online. Some sites also may compare prices offered at stores in your area. If you decide to buy online, keep shipping costs and delivery time in mind.

- *Carefully consider bargain offers* that are based on purchases of additional merchandise. For example, *Buy one, get one free* or *Free gift with purchase*. If you don't really want or need the item, it's not a deal.

- *Ask about refund and return policies for sale items.* Merchants may have different refund and return policies for sale items, especially clearance merchandise.

- *Ask about warranties.* Most items have some sort of guarantee. Also, some stores will extend the warranty or offer an extended warranty for you to purchase. Decide if this is necessary for the product you are buying. Many times it's not.

C Based on the reading, make a list of eight things you should do before you make a large purchase.

1. _____
2. _____
3. _____
4. _____
5. _____
6. _____
7. _____
8. _____

D Think about a large purchase that you have made. Put a check next to each of the tips in exercise C that you used before making that purchase.

E Where would you get information about a product before buying it? What factors would you consider? Complete the chart below. Then share your answers with a group and explain your reasons.

Product	Where I would get information	What I would consider
	TV/audio store Newspaper ads Internet	Good picture and sound Size of screen Warranty

F **Active Task:** Go to the library for a book or magazine or use the Internet to find a web site that gives advice to consumers before they buy.

| GOAL ▶ Use contrary-to-fact conditionals | *Grammar* |

A Contrary-to-fact conditionals express a condition and a result that are not true at this point in time. Study the examples below. Can you find the condition and the result in each of the statements?

EXAMPLES:

If I were rich, I would buy a new car. (*I'm not really rich, so I can't buy a new car.*)

If they had a million dollars, they would move to Beverly Hills. (*They don't have a million dollars, so they can't move to Beverly Hills.*)

B Study the chart below with your teacher.

Contrary-to-fact conditionals	
Condition (*if* + past tense verb)	**Result (*would* + base verb)**
If she *got* a raise,	she *would buy* a new house.
If they *didn't spend* so much money on rent,	they *would have* more money for entertainment.
If I *were* a millionaire,	I'd give all my money to charity.
If John *weren't* so busy at work,	he *would spend* more time with his children.

Contrary-to-fact (or unreal) conditional statements are sentences that are not true. The *if* clause can come in the first or second part of the sentence. In written English, use *were* (instead of *was*) for *if* clauses with first- and third-person singular forms of *be*. Notice how commas are used in the examples below.

C Complete the sentences with the correct verb forms.

1. If Bita _____ (be) an architect in the United States, she _____ (design) beautiful homes.

2. If the Petersons both _____ (retire), they _____ (travel) around the world.

3. Van _____ (buy) a new computer if she _____ (have) some extra money.

4. If my husband _____ (be) rich, he _____ (buy) me an expensive diamond ring.

5. George _____ (save) more money if he _____ (not spend) so much on eating out.

6. You _____ (not be) so tired if you _____ (have) more time to relax.

D **Study the chart with your teacher.**

Wh- question	*Yes/no* question
what + *would* + subject + base verb + *if* + subject + past tense	*would* + subject + base verb + *if* + subject + past tense
What would you do if you won the lottery?	Would you give up your job if you won the lottery?

E **Work in groups. Take turns asking your group the questions below. Each person must answer with a conditional statement.**

EXAMPLE:
Student A: What would you do if you won the lottery?
Student B: If I won the lottery, I'd give up my job.
Student C: If I won the lottery, I'd buy a house.
Student D: If I won the lottery, I'd travel round the world.

What would you do if . . .

1. _____ you had a million dollars?

2. _____ you lived in a mansion?

3. _____ you had your own airplane?

4. _____ you were the boss of a huge company?

5. _____ you owned an island in the Pacific?

6. _____ (your own idea)

F **Write three personal statements about what you would do if your financial situation were different.**

1. _____

2. _____

3. _____

Charge it!

GOAL ▶ Interpret credit card information

Life skill

A Fill out the credit card application below with all of your basic information. If you don't want to use your real information in your book, you can make it up.

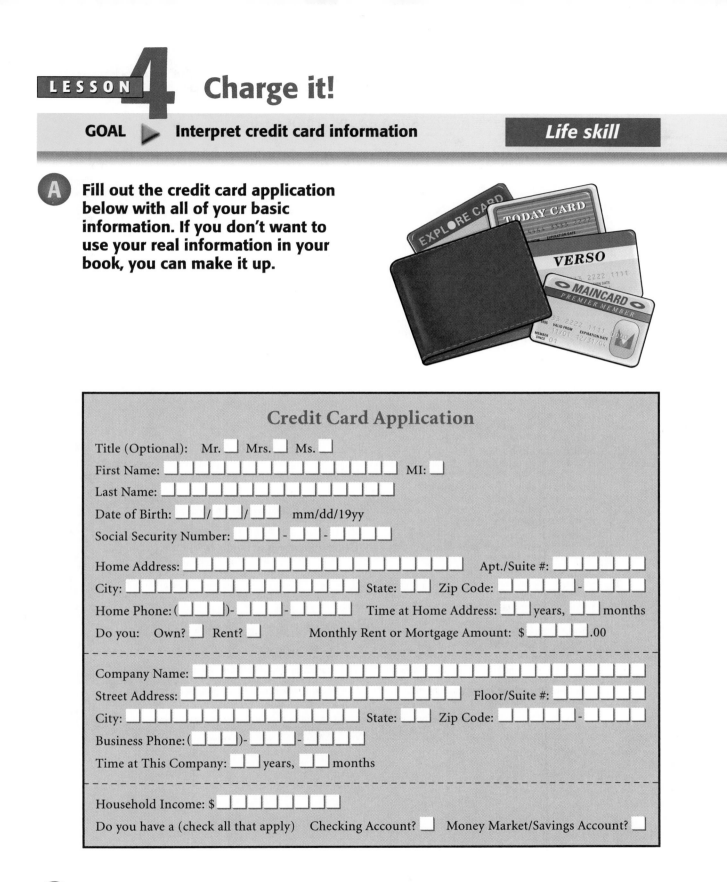

Credit Card Application

Title (Optional): Mr. ☐ Mrs. ☐ Ms. ☐

First Name: ☐☐☐☐☐☐☐☐☐☐☐☐☐☐☐☐☐☐ MI: ☐

Last Name: ☐☐☐☐☐☐☐☐☐☐☐☐☐☐☐☐

Date of Birth: ☐☐/☐☐/☐☐ mm/dd/19yy

Social Security Number: ☐☐☐ - ☐☐ - ☐☐☐☐

Home Address: ☐☐☐☐☐☐☐☐☐☐☐☐☐☐☐☐☐☐☐☐☐ Apt./Suite #: ☐☐☐☐☐☐

City: ☐☐☐☐☐☐☐☐☐☐☐☐☐☐☐ State: ☐☐ Zip Code: ☐☐☐☐☐-☐☐☐☐

Home Phone: (☐☐☐)- ☐☐☐-☐☐☐☐ Time at Home Address: ☐☐years, ☐☐months

Do you: Own? ☐ Rent? ☐ Monthly Rent or Mortgage Amount: $☐☐☐☐☐.00

Company Name: ☐☐☐☐☐☐☐☐☐☐☐☐☐☐☐☐☐☐☐☐☐☐☐☐☐

Street Address: ☐☐☐☐☐☐☐☐☐☐☐☐☐☐☐☐☐☐☐☐ Floor/Suite #: ☐☐☐☐☐☐

City: ☐☐☐☐☐☐☐☐☐☐☐☐☐☐☐ State: ☐☐ Zip Code: ☐☐☐☐☐-☐☐☐☐

Business Phone: (☐☐☐)- ☐☐☐-☐☐☐☐

Time at This Company: ☐☐years, ☐☐months

Household Income: $☐☐☐☐☐☐☐☐☐

Do you have a (check all that apply) Checking Account? ☐ Money Market/Savings Account? ☐

B Do you have a credit card? What kind of card is it? What is the interest rate? What do you use it for? Discuss these questions with your group.

C Read the following information about credit cards.

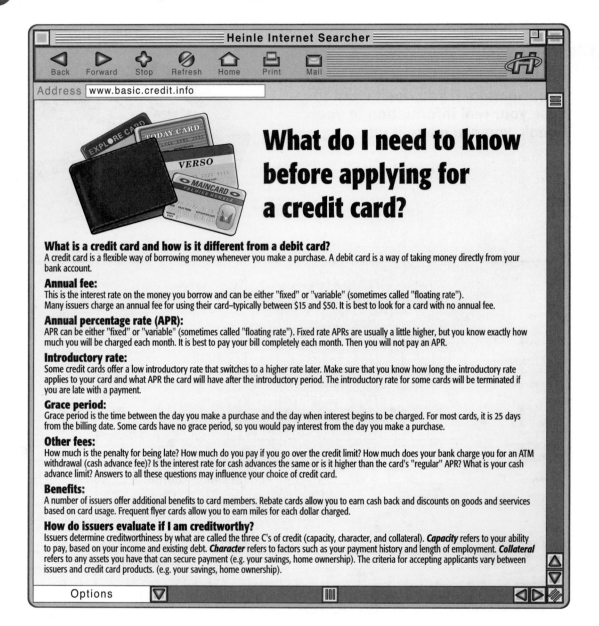

Heinle Internet Searcher

◁ Back   ▷ Forward   ✛ Stop   ⊘ Refresh   ⌂ Home   🖨 Print   ✉ Mail

Address: www.basic.credit.info

What do I need to know before applying for a credit card?

What is a credit card and how is it different from a debit card?
A credit card is a flexible way of borrowing money whenever you make a purchase. A debit card is a way of taking money directly from your bank account.

Annual fee:
This is the interest rate on the money you borrow and can be either "fixed" or "variable" (sometimes called "floating rate").
Many issuers charge an annual fee for using their card–typically between $15 and $50. It is best to look for a card with no annual fee.

Annual percentage rate (APR):
APR can be either "fixed" or "variable" (sometimes called "floating rate"). Fixed rate APRs are usually a little higher, but you know exactly how much you will be charged each month. It is best to pay your bill completely each month. Then you will not pay an APR.

Introductory rate:
Some credit cards offer a low introductory rate that switches to a higher rate later. Make sure that you know how long the introductory rate applies to your card and what APR the card will have after the introductory period. The introductory rate for some cards will be terminated if you are late with a payment.

Grace period:
Grace period is the time between the day you make a purchase and the day when interest begins to be charged. For most cards, it is 25 days from the billing date. Some cards have no grace period, so you would pay interest from the day you make a purchase.

Other fees:
How much is the penalty for being late? How much do you pay if you go over the credit limit? How much does your bank charge you for an ATM withdrawal (cash advance fee)? Is the interest rate for cash advances the same or is it higher than the card's "regular" APR? What is your cash advance limit? Answers to all these questions may influence your choice of credit card.

Benefits:
A number of issuers offer additional benefits to card members. Rebate cards allow you to earn cash back and discounts on goods and seervices based on card usage. Frequent flyer cards allow you to earn miles for each dollar charged.

How do issuers evaluate if I am creditworthy?
Issuers determine creditworthiness by what are called the three C's of credit (capacity, character, and collateral). *Capacity* refers to your ability to pay, based on your income and existing debt. *Character* refers to factors such as your payment history and length of employment. *Collateral* refers to any assets you have that can secure payment (e.g. your savings, home ownership). The criteria for accepting applicants vary between issuers and credit card products. (e.g. your savings, home ownership).

Options ▽   ▥   ◁▷

D What did you learn from the article about the following words? Discuss them with your class.

annual fee	late fee	credit limit	introductory rate
grace period	annual percentage rate (APR)		creditworthiness

E Read the chart and decide which credit card is the best deal.

	Verso	Maincard	Explore Card (must pay in full each month)	Todaycard
Annual Fee	$20	$15	$55	$0
APR	15%	14.9%	NA	21%
Introductory Rate (6 months)	2.9%	0%	3.8%	9.9%
Late Fee	$20	$10	$50	$25
Benefits	none	airline miles (1 for each dollar you spend)	none	cash back (1% of purchases)

F Which card did you choose? Why?

_____

_____

G What are the advantages and disadvantages of having a credit card? Discuss with your group.

 H **Active Task:** Find a real credit card application and fill it out. (Don't send it in unless you really want the card!)

GOAL ▶ Interpret loan information   *Life skill*

A   Todd and Sara are thinking of buying a house. Todd is worried about money, so he made an appointment with a financial planner to talk about a mortgage. Look at the expressions below and discuss them with your teacher. Then listen to Todd talking with the financial planner.

| mortgage | down payment | price range | credit check | deposit |
| afford | get approved for a loan | financial commitment | purchase price |

B   Listen to the first part of the conversation again. What are the three questions Todd must ask himself? Write them below.

1. _____
2. _____
3. _____

C   What are the next steps Todd must take? Listen to what the financial planner says and write the four steps below.

1. _____
2. _____
3. _____
4. _____

D   Todd will need to give the financial planner six things. Do you remember what they are? Write them below. If you can't remember, listen again.

1. _____
2. _____
3. _____
4. _____
5. _____
6. _____

E   Imagine you are trying to get a mortgage and you have to gather all of the items listed above. Put a check next to each one that you have at home right now.

F **Read the information about loans.**

When you decide to purchase something that costs more than you can pay for right now, you can put it on your credit card, or you can get a loan. A loan from a bank or lending institution is something you have to apply for directly. You usually have to specify the amount and what kind of purchase you want to make. For large purchases, you usually need collateral, such as your house, your business, or a down payment. The interest rate will vary according to the amount you borrow, where you borrow the money from, and your creditworthiness.

G **With a partner, discuss the differences between these purchasing options. Make notes in the chart below.**

Loan	Credit card

H **Look at the list of items below. Next to each one, decide if you should get a loan or put it on a credit card. Compare your answers with a group and explain why.**

	Car	College course	Computer	TV	Airline ticket	Small business
loan						
credit card						

LESSON 6 How they pull you in

GOAL ▶ Analyze advertising techniques

Life skill

A Look at the following ads for cameras.

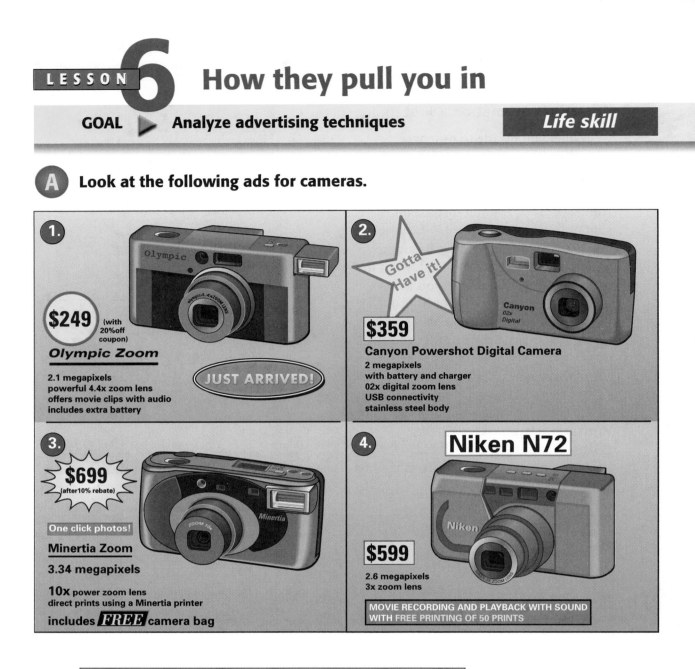

1. **Olympic Zoom** — $249 (with 20%off coupon)
2.1 megapixels
powerful 4.4x zoom lens
offers movie clips with audio
includes extra battery
JUST ARRIVED!

2. Gotta Have it! **Canyon Powershot Digital Camera** — $359
2 megapixels
with battery and charger
02x digital zoom lens
USB connectivity
stainless steel body

3. $699 (after 10% rebate) **Minertia Zoom**
One click photos!
3.34 megapixels
10x power zoom lens
direct prints using a Minertia printer
includes **FREE** camera bag

4. **Niken N72** — $599
2.6 megapixels
3x zoom lens
MOVIE RECORDING AND PLAYBACK WITH SOUND
WITH FREE PRINTING OF 50 PRINTS

> pixels – tiny squares that make up a digital image
>
> megapixel – one million pixels
>
> zoom – a zoom lens makes an image appear close up

B Discuss these questions with your group.

1. Which ad is most attractive? Why?
2. What kind of information do the ads give?
3. What information is not included?
4. How do the ads try to persuade you to buy?

C Look at the ads on the previous pages to complete the table below.

	Olympic	Canyon	Minertia	Niken
Price	$249			
Coupon or rebate needed?		no		
Zoom			10x	
Pixels				2.6 million
Features	offers movie clips with audio			
Special Offers			free camera bag	

D Is there more information you'd like to know about the cameras? Write three questions below that you might ask a salesperson.

1. _____

2. _____

3. _____

E Discuss these questions with your group.

1. What do advertisers do to get you interested in their products?

2. Can you always trust advertisements?

3. What's the best way to find out the truth about a product?

F Based on the advertisements, which camera would you buy? Why?

 G **Active Task:** Look at some digital camera ads in the newspaper or on the Internet. How do they compare to the ads in your book?

Express yourself

A Tell the class about a time when you complained about a product or service.

B Look at each of the situations below. With a partner, decide who you would talk to and what you would say, and what you would like to see happen.

1. You got home from the grocery store and realized the milk is bad.

   Who would you talk to? _____ *grocery store manager* _____

   What would you say? _____ *I just got home and realized this milk is bad.* _____

   What would you like to see happen? _____ *I would like a new carton of milk.* _____

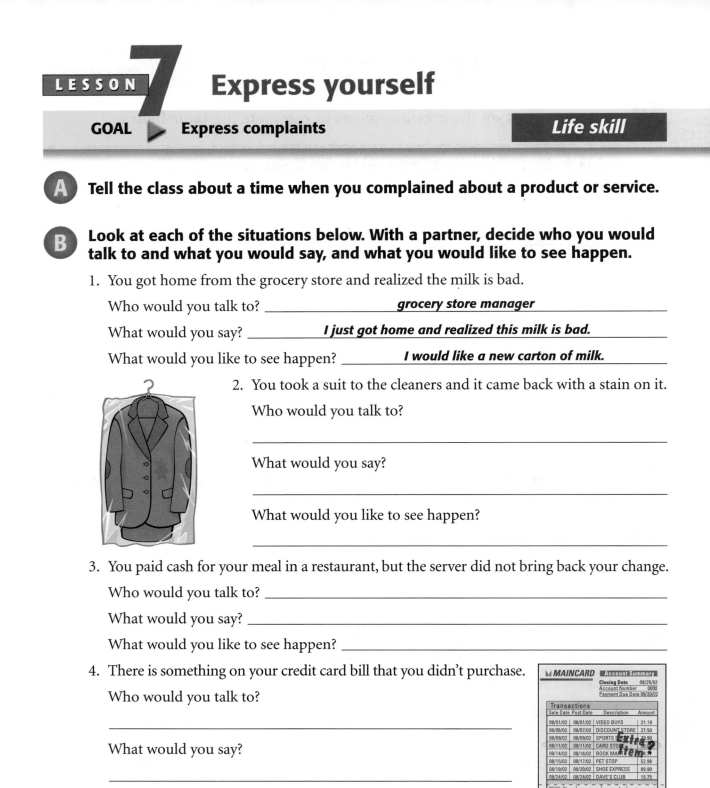

2. You took a suit to the cleaners and it came back with a stain on it.

   Who would you talk to?

   _____

   What would you say?

   _____

   What would you like to see happen?

   _____

3. You paid cash for your meal in a restaurant, but the server did not bring back your change.

   Who would you talk to? _____

   What would you say? _____

   What would you like to see happen? _____

4. There is something on your credit card bill that you didn't purchase.

   Who would you talk to?

   _____

   What would you say?

   _____

   What would you like to see happen?

   _____

   _____

C With your partner, choose one of the topics above and write a conversation between the two people. Practice your conversation and present it to the class.

D **One of the most effective ways to complain is to write a business letter. Read the letter below.**

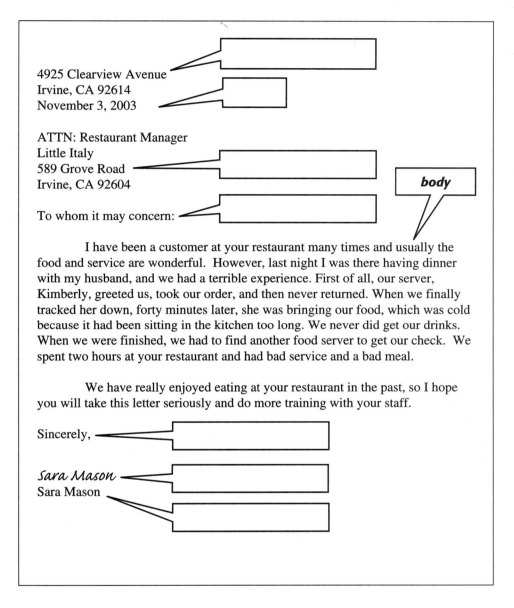

4925 Clearview Avenue
Irvine, CA 92614
November 3, 2003

ATTN: Restaurant Manager
Little Italy
589 Grove Road
Irvine, CA 92604

To whom it may concern:

body

     I have been a customer at your restaurant many times and usually the food and service are wonderful. However, last night I was there having dinner with my husband, and we had a terrible experience. First of all, our server, Kimberly, greeted us, took our order, and then never returned. When we finally tracked her down, forty minutes later, she was bringing our food, which was cold because it had been sitting in the kitchen too long. We never did get our drinks. When we were finished, we had to find another food server to get our check. We spent two hours at your restaurant and had bad service and a bad meal.

     We have really enjoyed eating at your restaurant in the past, so I hope you will take this letter seriously and do more training with your staff.

Sincerely,

Sara Mason
Sara Mason

E **Answer the questions about the letter.**

1. Who is Sara complaining to? _____

2. What is she complaining about? _____

3. What do you think will happen? _____

_____

F Use the words below to label the parts of the business letter on the previous page.

- return address
- date
- inside address
- greeting/salutation
- ~~body~~
- closing
- typed/printed name
- signature

G A business letter should contain the following information. Look at Sara's letter again. Did she mention all of these in her letter?

- who you are
- why you are writing
- an explanation of the problem or situation
- a resolution

H Choose one of the situations below and write a business letter to make a complaint. Remember to format the letter correctly and include all of the necessary information.

Company	Reason for letter
1. Lane's Accessories 8695 Tiguk Ave. Sioux Falls, SD 57104	The purse you bought is falling apart after one month.
2. Media Vision 4679 Lolly Lane Long Beach, CA 90745	You were charged for two months of cable instead of one.
3. Riverview Bank 47986 Washington Ave Grand Rapids, MI 49503	There is a charge on your credit card statement that doesn't belong to you.
4. Produce World 875 7th Ave New York, NY 10011	You were treated poorly by an employee.
5. Your own idea	Your own idea

Review

A Look back at page 17 and review how to make vocabulary cards. Choose four new words that you learned in this unit and write them below. Make a vocabulary card for each word or expression.

1. _____   3. _____

2. _____   4. _____

B You have just inherited $100,000 from a relative who passed away. What would you do with it? Write three conditional statements about the possibilities. Then share your answers with the class.

1. _____

2. _____

3. _____

C Complete each of the following questions.

1. What would you do if _____

2. What would you buy if _____

3. What would you take with you if _____

D Now ask three people in your class each of these questions and write their answers below. Share their answers with the class.

Question	Student 1	Student 2	Student 3
No. 1			
No. 2			
No. 3			

E Decide if each statement below is true or false based on what you learned in this unit. On a separate piece of paper, take each false statement and make it a true statement.

____ 1. A smart consumer asks a lot of questions about a product before buying it.

____ 2. Advertisements always tell you everything about the product.

____ 3. Budgets are only for people with a lot of money.

____ 4. Getting a loan isn't a long-term financial commitment.

____ 5. It is better to pay your credit card balance every month.

____ 6. Sometimes, credit cards carry high interest rates.

____ 7. Writing a business letter is a good way to express a complaint.

____ 8. You must have a credit card to buy an expensive item.

F Imagine that your family of four has $3,000 to live on per month. Realistically, how would you budget your money? Fill in the chart below.

Expense	Budgeted amount
Rent/Mortgage payment	
Utilities: Gas/Electricity	
Auto: Car payment/Gas/Insurance	
Food	
Medical	
Clothing	
Cable/Phone/Internet	
Entertainment	
Savings	
TOTAL	$3,000

G With a group, make a list of the things you need to think about and do before you purchase an expensive item. Compare your list with another group and add any new ideas to your list.

H Imagine you are writing an advertisement for a product. What information should be included in your ad? Make a list and share it with the class.

TEAM PROJECT

Create a purchasing plan

With a team, you will create a purchase plan for a large item.

1. Form a team with four or five students. Choose positions for each member of your team.

Position	Job Description	Student Name
Student 1 Leader	See that everyone speaks English. See that everyone participates.	
Student 2 Secretary	Take notes and write purchase plan.	
Student 3 Designer	Design ad for product and purchase plan layout.	
Students 4/5 Member (s)	Help secretary and designer with their work.	

2. Think of a large item that you would like to purchase.

3. Create an advertisement for this product.

4. Write down all the steps you will need to take to purchase this item. (Hint: budget, comparison shopping, ads, loan information)

5. Write a brief description of how you will do each step.

6. Design a purchase plan document that has a space for the ad, each step in your purchase plan, and artwork.

7. Present what you've created to the class.

PRONUNCIATION

Word Linking. Listen to sentences 1–3 and notice how the word ending in /w/ is linked to the following word in each sentence. Then listen to sentences 4–6. Listen to how the /w/ sound is introduced to link words. Listen again and repeat. Make new sentences using this type of word linking.

1. How often do you make large purchases?

2. What do you know about personal finance?

3. Now is the time to check out our special offers.

4. I want to apply for a credit card.

5. It is so easy to borrow money.

6. Go online to check our prices.

LEARNER LOG

In this unit, you learned many things about personal finance. How comfortable do you feel doing each of the skills listed below? Rate your comfort level on a scale of 1 to 4.
1 = Not so comfortable **2** = Need more practice **3** = Comfortable **4** = Very comfortable
If you circle 1 or 2, write down the page number where you can review this skill.

Life Skill	Comfort Level				Page(s)
I can calculate monthly expenses.	1	2	3	4	_____
I can plan a monthly budget.	1	2	3	4	_____
I know how to be a smart consumer.	1	2	3	4	_____
I can fill out a credit card application.	1	2	3	4	_____
I can listen to information about loans.	1	2	3	4	_____
I can discuss purchasing options.	1	2	3	4	_____
I can analyze advertising techniques.	1	2	3	4	_____
I can express consumer complaints.	1	2	3	4	_____

Grammar

I can use contrary-to-fact conditionals.	1	2	3	4	_____

Academic Skill

I can read consumer purchasing information.	1	2	3	4	_____
I can read and evaluate credit card information.	1	2	3	4	_____
I can compare numerical data and organize information.	1	2	3	4	_____
I can write a business letter.	1	2	3	4	_____

Reflection
Complete the following statements with your thoughts from this unit.

I learned _____

I would like to find out more about _____

I am still confused about _____

UNIT 3

Buying a Home

GOALS

- Interpret housing advertisements
- Use comparative and superlative adjectives
- Use comparative and superlative questions
- Use *yes/no* and information questions
- Write a letter to a real estate agent
- Interpret a bar graph
- Understand steps in a process

LESSON 1

The American dream

GOAL ▶ Interpret housing advertisements   *Vocabulary*

A Read the following advertisements from *Homes for Sale.* Write the names from the box with the correct description.

HOMES FOR SALE

Cozy two-bedroom, two-bath single family home. Located in a secluded neighborhood, far from city life.

You won't believe this price for a house in this area. Working fireplace. Big yard. Excellent seasonal views. Must sell. Come see and make an offer now!
$120,000

★★★★★★★★★★

Single-family 4-bedroom, 3-bath, 1500 sq. ft. home with an added family room.
Location is great!
Near jobs, bus, and schools. You must see this home and area. Amenities: pool, fireplace, central a/c, master suite and big yard!
Let's negotiate!
Asking price
$225,000

RENTAL SALES

You'd think this 1000-square-foot condo was brand new! **Located in the heart** of Los Angeles, near all the nightlife you could imagine. Seller just added new carpet, paint, new faucets and sinks, and beautiful ceramic tile flooring. Two master suites, laundry room, underground parking, balcony with spectacular views. This condo will not last long on the market, *so hurry!*
$200,000

Downtown
Condo

Country
Cottage

Suburban
Dream

B **What do you think the following words from the ads could mean? Is there more than one meaning?**

cozy _____   secluded _____

near nightlife _____   seasonal views _____

C **Find each of the vocabulary words in the ads and try to work out the meaning using the context.**

asking price	offer	amenities	market	negotiate

D **Complete the following chart by looking at the *Homes for Sale* ads.**

	Type of property	Size	Asking price	Number of bedrooms	Number of bathrooms	Location	Amenities
Country Cottage							big yard
Suburban Dream	single family home						
Downtown Condominium		1000 sq.ft.					

E **Using the ads on the previous page as examples, write an advertisement for the place you live on a separate piece of paper.**

F **Active Task:** Read some housing ads in the newspaper or on the Internet. Make a list of any words or abbreviations you don't understand and try to work out the meanings.

LESSON 2 Bigger? Better?

GOAL ▶ Use comparative and superlative adjectives · *Grammar*

A Listen to Joey and Courtney discuss two properties that Courtney looked at. As you listen, take notes about the *advantages* and *disadvantages* of each place.

House	Advantages	Disadvantages
Condominium		

B With a partner, compare the house and the condominium.

EXAMPLE:
Student A: What is the advantage of living in the house?
Student B: The house is quieter than the condo and you have more space.

C Which one would you rather live in? Why? Write a paragraph.

_____

_____

_____

_____

_____

_____

_____

_____

D Review comparative and superlative adjectives by completing the chart below.

Adjective	Comparative	Superlative
beautiful		
noisy		
safe		
comfortable		
far		
hot		
friendly		
bad		
cheap		
dark		
spacious		
flat		

* Note: Some two-syllable adjectives have two forms: e.g., *quieter* or *more quiet.*

E Which of the adjectives above correspond to the rules below?

1. Add *-er* or *-est* to a one-syllable adjective. _____

2. Use *more* or *most* before adjectives of two or more syllables. _____

3. Add *–r* to one-syllable adjectives that end in *e*. _____

4. Change *y* to *i* and add *-er* or *-est*. _____

5. These adjectives have irregular forms. _____

6. Double the final consonant of adjectives ending in consonant-vowel-consonant and add *-er* or *-est*.

_____

F Find opposites for each adjective in the chart above. Write the comparative and superlative form of each new adjective on a separate piece of paper.

G With a partner, describe the place you are living in now and compare it to the place you used to live, using the adjectives above.

EXAMPLE: I used to live in a small one-bedroom apartment with uncomfortable furniture. But now I live in a bigger apartment with the most comfortable couch!

Which one is safer?

GOAL ▶ **Use comparative and superlative questions** | *Grammar*

What are Sara and
Courtney discussing?
What do you think they
are saying?

A **Sara and Courtney have been comparing notes on houses they've looked at. Listen to their conversation.**

Courtney: Have you looked at any new houses this week?
Sara: Yes, I saw three places the other day. Look at this brochure!
Courtney: The Country Cottage, the Suburban Dream, and the Downtown Condo. I like the
sound of the Country Cottage best. It sounds more comfortable than the others.
Sara: Yeah, and it's the closest to where we live now.
Courtney: Oh really? Which place is the safest?
Sara: Actually, I think the Suburban Dream is the safest.
Courtney: Which one has the biggest floor plan?
Sara: The Suburban Dream. That would be ideal for our family.
Courtney: Is it the most expensive?
Sara: Of course! I have expensive taste.

B **What questions does Courtney ask? How does Sara answer her? Discuss as a class.**

C **Practice the conversation with a partner.**

D **Study the charts with your teacher.**

Questions using comparative and superlative adjectives				
Question word	Subject	Verb	Adjective or noun	Rule
Which	one place house	is	*bigger?* *closer* to work? the *safest?*	Use *be* when following with an adjective.
		has	*more* rooms? *the biggest* floor plan?	Use *have* before a noun.

Answers			
Question	Short answer	Long answer	Rule
Which one is *bigger,* the condominium or the house?	The condominium.	The condominium *is bigger.* The condominium *is bigger than* the house.	When talking about two things, and mentioning both of them, use *than.*
Which place has *more rooms?*	The house.	The house *has more rooms.* The house *has more rooms than* the condominium.	When talking about two things, but only mentioning one of them, **do not** use *than.*

E **What are some adjectives used to describe homes? What are some nouns used to describe homes? Make two lists on a separate sheet of paper.**

Adjectives	Nouns
safe	*great location*
spacious	*big yard*

F **Using the information about the three properties on page 41, practice this conversation with different students in the class. Use the adjectives and nouns from your lists.**

Student A: Have you looked at any new houses this week?

Student B: Actually, I looked at three places the other day.

Student A: Oh really? Which place is/has _____?

Student B: The _____ is/has _____.

G Listen to the four advertisements for *Homes for Sale* and fill in the information you hear.

Prince's Palace	Fixer-Upper	City High-Rise	Rural Residence
Price: _____	Price: _____	Price: _____	Price: _____
Size: _____	Size: _____	Size: _____	Size: _____
Neighborhood: _____	Neighborhood: _____	Neighborhood: _____	Neighborhood: _____
Amenities: _____ _____ _____	Amenities: _____ _____ _____	Amenities: _____ _____ _____	Amenities: _____ _____ _____

H Write four comparative and superlative questions about the homes above.

EXAMPLE:
__Which place has the best amenities?__

1. _____

2. _____

3. _____

4. _____

I With a partner, practice asking and answering the questions in exercise H.

J Which home would you like to live in? Why? Tell your group.

4 Housing preferences

GOAL ▶ Use *yes/no* and information questions   *Grammar*

A Think about the following questions as you listen to the story about the Bwarie family.

1. Why is the Bwarie family looking for a new home?

2. What are they looking for in a new home?

The Bwarie family has outgrown their apartment. They have three children and a baby on the way and they are now renting a two-bedroom house. They've been putting away money every month from their paychecks and finally have enough money for a 10% down payment on a house. Every Sunday, the whole family piles into the car and they go look at properties for sale in the $100,000 to $120,000 price range. Until now, they have been doing this on their own. But now it's time to find a real estate agent.

However, before they meet with a real estate agent, they need to decide exactly what they want. Courtney and Joey Bwarie have thought long and hard about what they want to purchase. First of all, they want a house in a safe neighborhood that is within walking distance to their children's school. Second of all, they want four bedrooms, one for Courtney and Joey, one for the two boys, and another for their daughter and the baby girl who will be born next month. The fourth room will be used as an office for Courtney, who works from home. As far as bathrooms, four would be ideal, but they could survive with three if they had to. Some other things they would like are a big backyard for the children to play in and an attached two-car garage. Other amenities, such as air conditioning or a pool, are not important to them.

Now they know what they are looking for in a new home. That was the easy part. Finding a real estate agent, that's a different story!

B Read the story again and try to work out the meanings of the following words using the context.

survive	on the way	outgrown
pile into	ideal	putting away
real estate agent	within walking distance	down payment
thought long and hard	works from home	

C Go over the meanings with your teacher. Choose three words or expressions and write sentences.

D What are the Bwaries looking for in a home? Complete the checklist, based on the reading in exercise A.

Housing preferences checklist				
Features	**Yes**	**No**	**Features**	**Preference**
air conditioning	❏	❏	type of property	
backyard	❏	❏	number of bathrooms	
balcony	❏	❏	number of bedrooms	
garage	❏	❏	location	
elevator	❏	❏	price range	
pool	❏	❏	down payment (%)	

E What information did the Bwaries not talk about? What do you think their preferences might be?

F When asking someone about their preferences, you can use *yes/no* questions. Study the chart below.

Yes/no questions and short answers		
Do you want	air conditioning? a backyard?	Yes, I do. No, I don't.
Do they need	a balcony? a garage?	Yes, they do. No, they don't.
Does the house have	heating? a pool?	Yes, it does. No, it doesn't.

G Practice asking *yes/no* questions with a partner based on the information in exercise D.

EXAMPLE:
Student A: Do they want air conditioning?
Student B: No, they don't.

H Information questions start with *who, what, where, when, why,* or *how.* Study the chart below.

Information questions			
Information	**Example questions**		
type of property	What type	of property	do you want? is it?
number of bathrooms	How many	bedrooms	do you want?
number of bedrooms		bathrooms	does it have?
location	Where		is it?
price range	What		is your price range?
down payment (percentage)	How much		can you put down?

I Practice asking information questions to a partner based on the information in exercise D.

EXAMPLE:
Student A: What type of property does the Bwarie family want?
Student B: They want a house.

J Complete your own checklist based on things you would want in a new home. Add some extra things that are not on the list.

Housing preferences checklist				
Features	**Yes**	**No**	**Features**	**Preference**
air conditioning	❏	❏	type of property	
backyard	❏	❏	number of bathrooms	
balcony	❏	❏	number of bedrooms	
garage	❏	❏	location	
elevator	❏	❏	type of heating	
pool	❏	❏	price range	
	❏	❏	down payment (%)	
	❏	❏		

GOAL ▶ **Write a letter to a real estate agent** *Life skill*

 What are some ways you can think of to look for a house? Make a list of ideas with a group.

B **Read the letter that Joey wrote to Paradise Realty.**

15236 Dahlia Avenue
Costa Mesa, CA 92627
February 13, 2003

Paradise Realty
9875 Timber Lane
Costa Mesa, CA 92627

Dear Paradise Realty,

My family has decided to purchase a new home and we would appreciate any information you can send us about homes for sale.

We are looking for a four-bedroom home. We would like to live in a safe neighborhood, close to our children's school. We would prefer a home with a big enclosed yard that our children can play in. We might want to build a pool in the future, but right now it is not a priority. Other amenities, such as air conditioning, central heating, and built-in closet space would be nice, but they are not essential. Our price range is between $100,000 and $120,000 and we are prepared to put down 10%.

Please contact me at the address above, or you may call me or my wife Courtney at (949) 555-2408. Thank you for your time.

Sincerely,

Joseph Bwarie
Joseph Bwarie

C   If you were looking for a house, what things would you tell your real estate agent? (Hint: Remember your preferences checklist.) Make a list.

Things to tell the real estate agent

D   In the last unit you learned about parts of a business letter. Look at the list below. Find each piece of information in the letter on the previous page and write the correct number next to the paragraph where you find the information.

1. Describe what you want.

2. Thank the person for their time.

3. Explain why you are writing the letter.

E   Now it's your turn. Imagine you are going to buy a new house and you are writing a letter to a real estate agent. Use the letter on the previous page as an example and the list you made in exercise D. Write your letter on a separate sheet of paper.

F   **Active Task:** Use the Internet or the newspaper to find out about real estate agents in your area. What kind of services do they offer? What kind of fees do they charge?

LESSON 6
Homeownership in the United States

GOAL ▶ Interpret a bar graph

Academic skill

A Study the bar graph. What vocabulary do you need to understand the information? Make a list and discuss it with your class.

Homeownership Rates by Citizenship Status of Householder for the United States and Regions

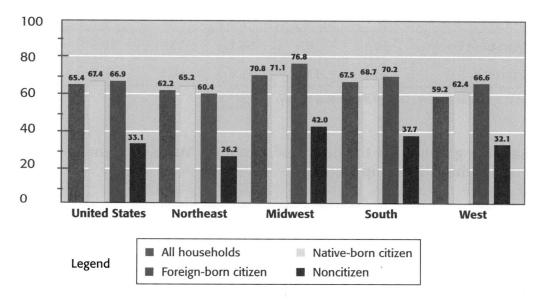

United States: 65.4, 67.4, 66.9, 33.1
Northeast: 62.2, 65.2, 60.4, 26.2
Midwest: 70.8, 71.1, 76.8, 42.0
South: 67.5, 68.7, 70.2, 37.7
West: 59.2, 62.4, 66.6, 32.1

Legend
■ All households   ☐ Native-born citizen
■ Foreign-born citizen   ■ Noncitizen

Source: U.S. Census Bureau, Current Population Survey

B Ask and answer questions about the bar graph with your partner.

EXAMPLES:
Student A: What percentage of households in the United States own their own homes?
Student B: 65.4% of households in the United States own their own homes.

Student B: What percentage of foreign-born citizens own their own homes in the United States?
Student A: 66.9% of foreign-born citizens own their own homes.

C Write two false statements and two true statements about the bar graph on a separate sheet of paper. Then ask your partner which are true and which are false. (Your partner cannot look at the graph.)

EXAMPLE:
Student A: In the West, more foreign-born citizens own their own homes than native-born citizens.
Student B: I think that's true.
Student A: Yes, it is true.

D Read the information in the chart below. What does it mean? Discuss it with your class.

Homeownership Rates by Citizenship Status and Age of Householder for the United States						
	United States	Under 35 years	35–44	45–54	55–64	65+
All households	65.4	39.1	65.5	75.6	80	78.9
Native-born citizens	67.4	41.1	67.9	77.1	81.5	80.2
Foreign-born citizens	66.9	38.5	64.1	75.4	78.5	72.3
Noncitizens	33.1	19.8	35.6	48.3	49.3	43.5

Source: U.S. Census Bureau, Current Population Survey

E Make a bar graph using the information above. Make sure you create a legend for the citizenship status.

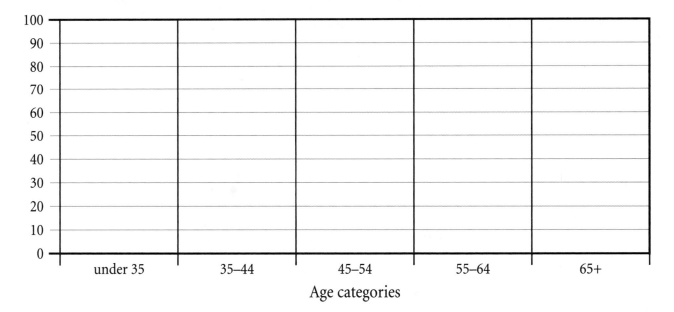

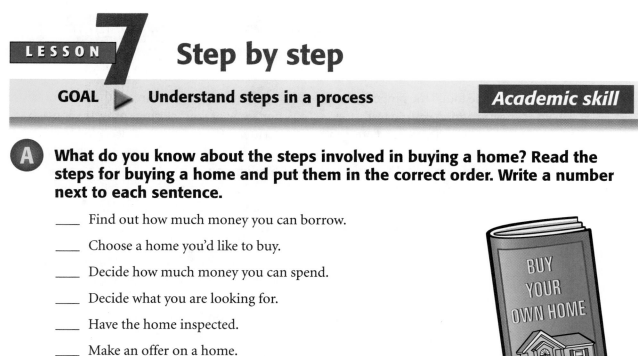

Step by step

GOAL ▶ Understand steps in a process   *Academic skill*

A **What do you know about the steps involved in buying a home? Read the steps for buying a home and put them in the correct order. Write a number next to each sentence.**

_____ Find out how much money you can borrow.

_____ Choose a home you'd like to buy.

_____ Decide how much money you can spend.

_____ Decide what you are looking for.

_____ Have the home inspected.

_____ Make an offer on a home.

_____ Move in.

_____ Negotiate until both parties come to an agreement.

_____ Start looking for homes in a neighborhood you'd like to live in.

B **Now read the article about home buying and check your answers.**

Buying a Home

Homebuyers can spend up to three months, and possibly more, looking for and purchasing a home. Their search begins by looking at housing ads, driving through neighborhoods they are interested in, and walking through open houses. Many first-time buyers will meet with a real estate agent to get help finding and buying a home.

Homebuyers should know how much they can afford. It isn't worth your time to look for a new home if you can't really afford to buy one. So it's a good idea to look at your financial situation first. You might be surprised at how much you can borrow, especially if the interest rates are good. Also, if you have some money saved for a down payment, your monthly payments may be lower than you think.

You should never make an offer on a home without looking at other houses in the same neighborhood. Just as you would comparison shop for a car or a computer, you should do a cost comparison on different homes for sale. You can do this by asking about the recent sales of similar properties. This information is available at local recorder's or assessor's offices, as well as through private companies or on the Internet. Also, if you can do some research on the seller, and his or her motivation for selling, it will put you in a better position. For instance, maybe the seller needs to sell quickly and would accept a low offer.

Once you have found the property that you want and can afford, you are ready to make an offer. A low-ball offer is an offer on a house that is a great deal less than the asking price. Unless the house is really overpriced, the seller will probably not accept a low-ball offer. Once you make an offer that is reasonable to the seller, he or she will either accept it or make a counter-offer. In this case, the negotiating process has begun. You may have to go back and forth three or four times before an agreement is reached.

Being a good negotiator can be tricky. Take your time when making your decision. This is a very important decision and you don't want to be rushed. Sometimes you can negotiate for repairs to the home before you move in, or you can ask the seller to pay for some of your closing costs. As soon as a written offer is made and accepted by both parties, the document becomes a legally binding contract.

Then the loan is processed by the lender (usually a bank) and the home is inspected. You should always have the home inspected. This will give you a chance to find out if anything is wrong that the seller didn't notify you of. After that, the final papers for the transfer of the title are prepared and any other last-minute business is taken care of. Finally, the closing takes place on a date agreed upon in the offer. On that date the title comes to you and soon you can enjoy your new home!

C **Find each of the following words in the article and match each vocabulary word/phrase with its correct meaning.**

____ 1. afford   a. a legal document

____ 2. contract   b. amount of money that the buyer is willing to pay for a house

____ 3. cost comparison   c. amount of money that the seller wants for the house

____ 4. negotiate   d. to look something over for problems or defects

____ 5. inspect   e. looking at different prices of homes

____ 6. lender   f. person or company that loans money

____ 7. asking price   g. the desire to do something

____ 8. motivation   h. date when the title to the house becomes yours

____ 9. offer   i. to have enough money to purchase something

____ 10. closing   j. discuss until you reach an agreement

D **What are the benefits of owning your own home? What are the drawbacks? Tell your partner.**

A **Read the housing advertisements and do the following activities with a partner.**

1. Always wanted to take a house and make it your own? Here's your chance! Settle into this 4-bedroom, 3.5 ba, 2,000 square foot fixer-upper. $150,000. Located in a busy neighborhood with lots of other families, this place is perfect for a young family.

2. Move out of the slow life and into the fast lane! A beautifully spacious 1,000 square foot studio apartment at the top of one of the city's newest high-rises is just what you're looking for. The building has 24-hour security. Utility room with washers and dryers is in the basement. The owner wants to lease it for $2000 a month but is willing to sell. Hurry! This one will go fast!

3. You've finally decided it's time to move out of the city and into the country. Well, we've got just the place for you. This three-bedroom rural residence is just what you need. It's a spacious 1,500 square foot ranch-style home with a huge backyard and a pool. It's located at the end of cul-de-sac where there are only five other homes. It is now being offered at $125,000.

1. Compare the three properties using comparative and superlative adjectives. Take turns making statements.

2. Ask each other *yes/no* and information questions based on the advertisements. Take turns asking questions.

3. Choose one of the ads and rewrite it to fit the description of a house you'd like to buy. Be prepared to read your ad to the class.

4. Describe the process of buying a home, using new words from this unit.

Review

B **Make a list of ten new vocabulary words that you learned in this unit.**

1. _____   6. _____
2. _____   7. _____
3. _____   8. _____
4. _____   9. _____
5. _____   10. _____

C **Choose three words and make vocabulary cards for them.**

EXAMPLE:

negotiate	
(verb)	
negotiation (noun)	negociar
negotiator (person)	(translation)

1. "Buyers commonly negotiate for better amenities."
2. To reach an agreement through discussion.
3. Negotiate until you reach an agreement.
4. We negotiated an agreement.

D **Complete the sentences below. Then read your answers to the rest of the class. The class will decide on the best answer.**

1. We need to write a business letter when _____

_____

2. We need to understand a bar graph when _____

_____

3. It is important to understand advertisements because _____

_____

4. We can use a preferences checklist when _____

_____

5. We use comparative adjectives when _____

_____

6. We use superlative adjectives when _____

_____

TEAM PROJECT

Buy your dream home

With a team, you will create a real estate brochure, choose properties that you are interested in, meet with a real estate agent, and decide which property to purchase.

1. Form a team with four or five students. Choose positions for each member of your team.

Position	Job Description	Student Name
Student 1 Leader	See that everyone speaks English. See that everyone participates.	
Student 2 Real Estate Agent	Take notes and write advertisements.	
Student 3 Graphic Designer	Design a brochure.	
Students 4/5 Member (s)	Help the real estate agent and the designer with their work.	

2. Create an imaginary real estate agency. What is the name of your agency? What type(s) of properties do you sell?

3. Choose three properties that your agency is trying to sell. Make up a brochure for these properties, including pictures and brief advertisements. Display your brochures around the room.

4. Now you are a family who wants to move to a new house. Decide what your housing preferences are and make a list.

5. From the brochures posted around the room, choose two properties that you are interested in, each one from a different agency.

6. Prepare a list of questions that you'd like to ask about each property.

7. In teams of two or three, set up appointments with the real estate agencies and meet with them about the properties you are interested in purchasing.

8. Report back to your group and make a decision about which property you'd like to make an offer on, comparing the information to your checklist.

9. Report your decision to the class.

PRONUNCIATION

Intonation Yes/no questions usually have a rising intonation. Information questions usually have a falling intonation. Listen to these examples. Underline the stressed words and draw arrows to show the intonation pattern that you hear.

1. Do you want a garage?
2. Do they need air conditioning?
3. Does it have a backyard?

4. What type of property do you want?
5. How many rooms does it have?
6. Where is it located?

LEARNER LOG

In this unit, you learned many things about buying a home. How comfortable do you feel doing each of the skills listed below? Rate your comfort level on a scale of 1 to 4.
1 = Not so comfortable **2** = Need more practice **3** = Comfortable **4** = Very comfortable
If you circle 1 or 2, write down the page number where you can review this skill.

Vocabulary	Comfort Level				Page(s)
I can interpret housing advertisements.	1	2	3	4	_____
I can use context clues to understand vocabulary.	1	2	3	4	_____
Life Skill					
I can write an advertisement.	1	2	3	4	_____
I can complete a housing preferences checklist.	1	2	3	4	_____
I can write a letter to a real estate agent.	1	2	3	4	_____
Grammar					
I can use comparative and superlative questions.	1	2	3	4	_____
I can use yes/no and information questions.	1	2	3	4	_____
Academic Skill					
I can organize information.	1	2	3	4	_____
I can interpret a bar graph.	1	2	3	4	_____
I can create a bar graph.	1	2	3	4	_____

Reflection
Complete the following statements with your thoughts from this unit.

I learned _____

I would like to find out more about _____

I am still confused about _____

Community

GOALS

- Identify resources in a community
- Use embedded questions
- Read a community bulletin board
- Identify and access library services
- Interpret a road map
- Volunteer in your community
- Interpret location/event descriptions

LESSON **1**

Your community

GOAL ▶ Identify resources in a community **Life skill**

A The Sanchez family has just bought a home in Loronado. They are trying to learn about all the available resources in their community. Which category does each place belong to? Make a list on a separate sheet of paper. Then think of one thing you can do at each place.

Education	Employment	Health	Local government	Recreation	Transportation
			City Clerk	Skate Park	

Community Resources

Balboa Park Museum	555-2939	71852 Orange Ave
Bus Transit	555-2678	35984 First Street
Chamber of Commerce	555-4671	72064 Orange Ave
~~City Clerk~~	555-8403	63246 Fifth Street #1
Department of Motor Vehicles	555-0013	54679 Fourth Street
Employment Development Department	555-5334	94678 Orange Ave
Health Clinic	555-8473	26489 First Street
High School	555-1238	34658 Loro Road
Hospital	555-7623	79346 Orange Ave
Little League Baseball	555-7300	66554 Third Street
Orange Adult School	555-9134	46589 Fourth Street
Public Library	555-0507	34661 Loro Road
Public Pool	555-4499	56321 Third Street
Senior Center	555-7342	97685 Sixth Street
~~Skate Park~~	555-6482	35211 Fourth Street
Superior Court	555-1796	96345 Orange Ave
Village Elementary School	555-8462	34660 Loro Road

Loronado Welcome Center

Where is Consuela?
What information can she find here?

B **Consuela Sanchez needs some help, so she's at the Loronado Welcome Center. Read the conversation below.**

Consuela: Hi. We just moved to Loronado and I'm looking for a place to <u>get a job</u>. Can you help me?

Receptionist: Of course. Why don't you try the <u>Employment Development Department</u>? It's located on <u>Orange Avenue</u>.

Consuela: Great! Thanks.

C **With a partner, practice the conversation above, but change the <u>underlined</u> information. Use the expressions below and the information on the previous page. There may be more than one possible answer.**

1. take some English classes
2. get a bus schedule
3. use a computer
4. volunteer
5. check out some books

6. get medical help
7. register my little boy for school
8. go swimming
9. look at some art
10. sign up for baseball

D **Now practice the same conversation, but this time ask about *your* town or city. Try to find a location and street for each activity above. Write down the information you find out. If your partner doesn't know, ask other students until you get an answer.**

E **Active Task:** Use the phone book or the Internet to find other locations to do the above activities. Report back to the class.

Can you tell me when the library opens?

GOAL ▶ **Use embedded questions**

Do you know if there is a library near here?

A **In each of the questions below, there are two questions. Can you find them? The first one has been done as an example.**

EXAMPLE:

Do you know if there is a library near here?

First question: ***Do you know?*** Second question: ***Is there a library near here?***

1. Can you show me where Orange Avenue is?

    First question: _____

    Second question: _____

2. Can you tell me when the post office opens?

    First question: _____

    Second question: _____

B **When two questions are combined, they are called *embedded questions*. One question is embedded in the other. Study the chart.**

Introductory question	Embedded question	Rule
Can you show me	where *Orange Avenue* is?	In an embedded question, the subject comes *before* the verb.
Do you know	if there <u>is</u> a library near here?	For *yes/no* questions, use *if* before the embedded question.
Can you tell me	when the library <u>opens</u>?	For questions with *do*, take out *do* and use the normal form of the verb.

Why do we use embedded questions? When you are talking to someone you don't know very well, it sounds more polite to put a question into a conversational phrase.

Expressions used to introduce embedded questions	
Could you tell me . . . ?	Would you show me . . . ?
Can you explain . . . ?	Do you know . . . ?

C **Change the following questions to embedded questions, using the expressions in the box.**

EXAMPLE:
What is the name of the local adult school?
Do you know what the name of the local adult school is?

1. What is the address of the public pool?
   _____

2. Where is Loronado?
   _____

3. Do you have running shoes?
   _____

4. What time does the library close?
   _____

5. Is Orange Adult School on this street?
   _____

6. How can I register for classes?
   _____

7. Where do you take your papers for recycling?
   _____

8. Is your restaurant open on Sunday?
   _____

D **On a separate sheet of paper, make a list of five questions you could ask a school counselor (using embedded questions). Examples: what classes to take, which colleges to transfer to, how to get a high school diploma.**

E **Active Task:** Make an appointment with a school counselor and ask him or her the questions you wrote. Then report back to the class.

Making suggestions

GOAL ▶ **Read a community bulletin board**   *Life skill*

Where are Consuela and her husband?
Who are they talking to?

A **Consuela and her husband, Ricardo, are talking to their next-door neighbors. Read their conversation.**

Ricardo: Let's find a good Italian restaurant. Can you think of where we could go?

Jim: Why don't we try this great little place called Island Pasta? It's a local hangout and the food is great!

Marie: I think they're closed tonight. How about going to Laredo's for a Mexican meal instead?

Consuela: Great idea!

B **With a partner, make new conversations. Use the topics below and suggestions from the chart. Follow the model in exercise A. Talk about places in your community.**

1. an inexpensive shoe store

2. a good movie for kids

3. a nice restaurant for your best friend's birthday dinner

4. a bookstore with a large selection of books

5. a good place to find really fresh fruit and vegetables

6. a place to eat Mexican food

7. a place to listen to good music

8. a bookstore to buy the required book for class

Suggestions	Responses
Why don't we . . . ?	Great idea!
We could . . .	Yes, let's do that!
How about . . . ?	Sure!
Do you want to . . . ?	No, I don't like that idea.
Let's . . .	Let's . . . instead.

Have you ever wanted to run a marathon?

Now's your chance! Run with a group of people just like you. Get advice from a group leader on fitness, health, and nutrition, and HAVE FUN! Call (777) 555-9768 for more info.

Basketball–Open Gym

The new downtown Recreation Center is where the action is! Come on down Monday and Wednesday afternoon, from 5-7 p.m. and join a game. Recreation Center, 4350 Third Street, (777) 555-6211

Did you hear your number?

B I N G O

Sunday nights starting 4 p.m. Call Charlene for more info (777) 555-9728

Lost Black Cat

Answers to the name of Blackie. Reward $50 If found, please call:

(777) 555-9617
(777) 555-9617
(777) 555-9617

Guitar Lessons

All levels
Must have a guitar
Music will be provided
Call to set up lessons
$20 a half hour

(777) 555-8697
(777) 555-8697
(777) 555-8697
(777) 555-8697
(777) 555-8697
(777) 555-8697

Summer Day Camp

Ages 3-6, 7-10, 11-14
Morning session 9-12 p.m.
Afternoon session 1-4 p.m.
June 25-August 24,
$60 a week per child.
Discounts available for more than one child.
Discounts available for morning and afternoon session.
See Activities Director to sign up.
Or call (777) 555-6211

C Read the notices on the community bulletin boards. Which notice is the most interesting to you? Why? Which notice is the least interesting to you? Why?

D Listen to the statements and write the correct number next to each notice.

COMMUNITY BULLETIN BOARD

Intro to T'ai Chi'
T'ai Chi Chih
Discover a wonderful form of exercise and meditation that is centuries old. Involve your mind, body, and spirit. All ages welcome.
Instructor: Mary Walker
Class Site: Room 209
Day: Thursday *Time:* 6 p.m.
Cost: $49/8 weeks
Begins September 4th

Arts and Crafts
Ever wanted to learn how to knit? Do needlepoint? Help your children with art projects? Make gifts for friends? Come join our craft group on Saturday mornings. There is a $5 material fee each day you attend. Come this Saturday! For more information, call Rick (777) 555-8693

Roommate wanted
Female, non-smoker, 1 bed, 1 bath, kitchen, garage $400 + sec deposit. Call Laura
Roommate (777) 555-9475
Roommate (777) 555-9475
Roommate (777) 555-9475

Summer Volleyball League
Got a group of people who want to play volleyball? Want to join a team that needs another player? Sign up for our summer volleyball league! All league games are on Thursday nights. For more information, call (777) 555-7809

Book Club
Do you like mysteries? Fiction? Romance? Non-fiction? Suspense? Come down to the Book Barn and join one of our Book clubs! Read a book every month and meet with others who share your passion to discuss it!
Book Barn, 4212 Loro Road, Tel. (777) 555-5630

E **Work in pairs. Student A, make a statement about one of the notices on the boards. Student B, respond with a suggestion.**

EXAMPLE:
Student A: I need a place to send my kids for the summer while I'm at work.
Student B: Why don't you phone the summer day camp?
Student A: That's a good idea.

F **Make a Community Bulletin Board in your classroom. Think of things you could offer and make flyers.**

G **Active Task:** Go to a community center and look at the bulletin board. Make a list of activities posted and report back to your class.

LESSON **4** **The public library**

GOAL ▶ **Identify and access library services**   *Life skill*

A **Discuss the following questions before you read.**

1. Have you been to your local library?

2. What services does it offer?

3. When is it open?

4. What kind of events are there?

B **Read the following information from the Loronado library brochure.**

LORONADO PUBLIC LIBRARY

The mission of the Loronado Public Library is to offer an extensive collection of books, audio-visual, and other library and information resources to meet the informational, recreational, and cultural needs of Loronado community members and to actively promote reading and lifelong learning.

Video Collection

We have an extensive video collection. You may check out two videos at a time for a two-week period.

Literacy Program

Do you know someone who needs help learning to read? The Loronado Public Library offers a free literacy program with personal tutors to help anyone at any age learn to read. Inquire at the front office for more information.

Computers

The library is online and you can have access to our entire catalogue of books as well as to the Internet. Use of computers is on a first-come, first-served basis and the time limit is 30 minutes when someone is waiting. Parents can be assured that we have computers in the children's reading room that are blocked from accessing inappropriate material.

Reading Room

Come visit the Reading Room where

children of all ages can read and check out books. Every Tuesday and Friday, we have Story Time where a different children's book will be read. Preschool at 10:30 a.m. Toddlers at 11:00 a.m.

Reference Section

Reference materials are books and journals that you can use while at the library. They may not be checked out.

Be a Volunteer

We're always looking for volunteers to help out in the library. If you have a few free hours to spare, join us!

Meeting Room

The Peterson Room is available for public meetings by reservation. Maximum seating 15.

C Study the floor plan of the Loronado Public Library.

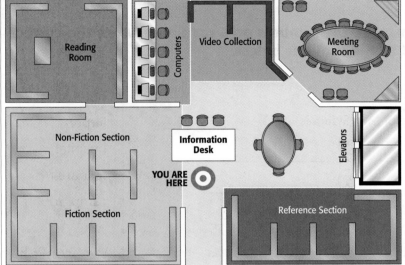

D Use the floor plan and the brochure to ask for and give information about the library.

EXAMPLE:

Student A: Where can I find a journal about computers?

Student B: Turn around and go straight ahead. That's our reference section.

E With a partner, brainstorm five questions you might ask a librarian. Write them down and share them with the class.

1. _____

2. _____

3. _____

4. _____

5. _____

F Of all the services listed on the pamphlet, which two are the most important to you? Why?

G **Active Task:** Visit your local library and find out about their services. Ask the librarian some of the questions you wrote above and report back to the class.

LESSON 5 How far is it?

GOAL ▶ Interpret a road map

Life skill

A A legend helps you read the symbols on a road map. Write the correct words from the box next to the symbols below.

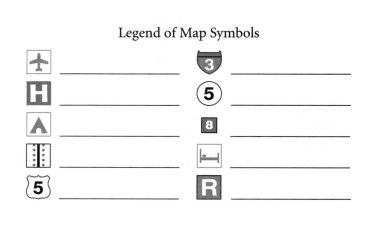

Legend of Map Symbols

✈ _____   ③ _____

H _____   ⑤ _____

▲ _____   8 _____

_____   🛏 _____

⑤ _____   R _____

| hotel/motel |
| airport |
| hospital |
| rest area |
| campground |
| exit |
| state scenic highway |
| freeway |
| interstate highway |
| state highway |

B Look at the map on the next page and answer the following questions with a partner.

1. Is there a hospital in Rose?

2. What interstate has rest stops?

3. Where is the nearest campground to Grandville?

4. Which highways are scenic?

5. Is there an airport near Lake Ellie?

C Look at the highway map scale below and estimate the road distances on the map.

1. How far is it from Grandville to Rose?

2. How far is it from Poppington to Lake Ellie?

3. How far is it from Loronado to Poppington?

4. How far is it from Lake Ellie to Rose?

5. How far is it from Grandville to Poppington?

6. How far is it from Rose to Loronado?

Highway Map Scale

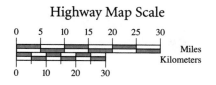

D **Listen to the following people giving directions. Where will the driver end up? Fill in the circle next to the correct answer.**

1. ○ Grandville   ○ Rose   ○ Lake Ellie   ○ Loronado   ○ Poppington
2. ○ Grandville   ○ Rose   ○ Lake Ellie   ○ Loronado   ○ Poppington
3. ○ Grandville   ○ Rose   ○ Lake Ellie   ○ Loronado   ○ Poppington
4. ○ Grandville   ○ Rose   ○ Lake Ellie   ○ Loronado   ○ Poppington

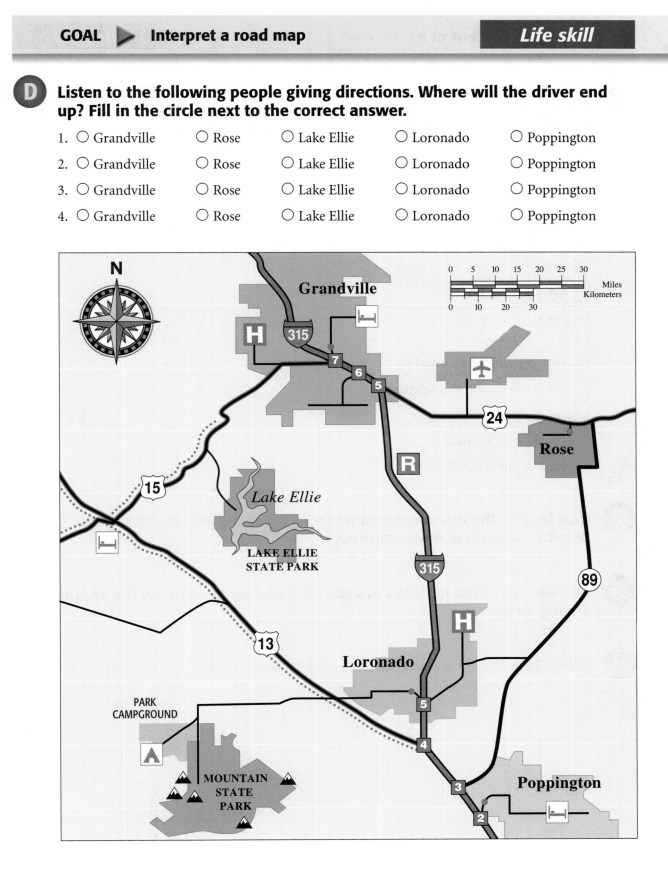

E **Now practice giving directions to a partner and receiving directions by writing them down. Student A, look at the map on the previous page to give directions to the places below. Student B, write down what your partner says. If you get confused, ask your partner to slow down or repeat. Then change roles.**

EXAMPLE:

From Rose to Grandville

Student A: I live in <u>Rose</u> and I need to get to <u>Grandville</u>. What's the best way to get there?

Student B: Take 24 West until it joins 315 North in Grandville. Follow 315 North and take Exit 7 off the Interstate.

Student A: About how far is it?

Student B: _____ miles.

Student A: Thank you so much.

1. From Poppington to Lake Ellie

2. From Loronado to Poppington

3. From Lake Ellie to Rose

4. From Rose to Loronado

5. From Grandville to Poppington

F **Now look at the directions you wrote down and compare them to the map. Did you write them down correctly?**

G **Choose one of the journeys in exercise E and try to estimate the approximate driving time.**

H **Active Task:** Call up your local supermarket or bookstore and ask for directions from your house. Write them down.

LESSON 6 Volunteering

GOAL ▶ **Volunteer in your community**   *Life skill*

A Have you ever offered to help a friend or neighbor do something? Do you belong to any local community organizations where you help out in some way? If you answered *yes* to any of the questions above, you are a volunteer!

B Before you can volunteer, you need to think about what you can do or like to do. Look at the list below and check the things that you can do or like to do. Add your own ideas to the list.

Skills	I can	I like to	My partner can	My partner likes to
ask for money				
build structures				
clean				
cook				
give a speech				
keep track of money				
make phone calls				
organize				
plan a meeting				
plan a party				
put books in alphabetical order				
spend time with children				
talk to people				
teach someone English				
teach someone to read				
teach someone math				
use the computer				
_____				
_____				

C Now interview your partner. Ask what he or she can and likes to do and put checks in the appropriate columns. Use the following questions:

Can you _____?

Do you like to _____?

D **Where are some places in your community you might be able to volunteer? With a group, make a list. Share your list with the class.**

Places to Volunteer

E **Now look back at the checklist for you and your partner. Come up with one or two places each of you might like to volunteer based on your skills. Give your partner suggestions.**

Places I can volunteer	Places my partner can volunteer
1.	1.
2.	2.

F **Now that you have two places you can volunteer, what's the next step? First of all, figure out how to contact them and find the person in charge of volunteering. Second, ask them if they need volunteers. If so, what type of help do they need? Third, find out what hours they need people.**

G **Come up with at least three questions you might ask when you visit or call the location.**

1. _____
2. _____
3. _____

H **Active Task:** Find the phone number and/or address of two places you might volunteer in your phone directory or on the Internet. Visit the location or call and talk to someone. Ask them your three questions. Volunteer to help!

Where can we get good French food?

GOAL ▶ Interpret location/event descriptions   *Life skill*

A Read the information from the Loronado Visitor's Guide.

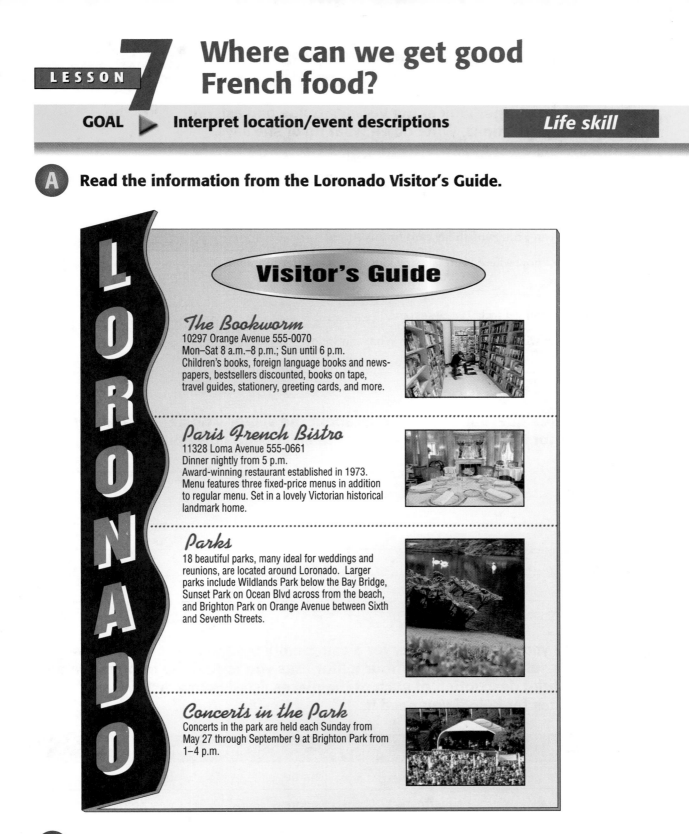

Visitor's Guide

The Bookworm
10297 Orange Avenue 555-0070
Mon–Sat 8 a.m.–8 p.m.; Sun until 6 p.m.
Children's books, foreign language books and news-papers, bestsellers discounted, books on tape, travel guides, stationery, greeting cards, and more.

Paris French Bistro
11328 Loma Avenue 555-0661
Dinner nightly from 5 p.m.
Award-winning restaurant established in 1973. Menu features three fixed-price menus in addition to regular menu. Set in a lovely Victorian historical landmark home.

Parks
18 beautiful parks, many ideal for weddings and reunions, are located around Loronado. Larger parks include Wildlands Park below the Bay Bridge, Sunset Park on Ocean Blvd across from the beach, and Brighton Park on Orange Avenue between Sixth and Seventh Streets.

Concerts in the Park
Concerts in the park are held each Sunday from May 27 through September 9 at Brighton Park from 1–4 p.m.

B Make a list of what type of information you can find in the descriptions.

_____   _____   _____
        address

_____   _____   _____

C **Have your partner look at the Visitor's Guide and ask him or her the following questions. Write down what he or she says.**

1. Where can I go for a delicious French meal? _____

2. I'm planning a wedding with a friend. Do you know of a good location?

   _____

3. Where can I find a birthday card for my mom? _____

4. Do you know where I can take my kids for some entertainment on Sunday?

   _____

5. Where can I get today's newspaper? _____

6. My sister will be here on April 23. What can we do? _____

   _____

D **Write three questions of your own about the Visitor's Guide and ask your partner for the information. Try to write embedded questions.**

Question: _____

Answer: _____

Question: _____

Answer: _____

Question: _____

Answer: _____

E **Imagine you are a staff writer for a community brochure that will be given to all the residents in your city. Your editor asks you to find the information and write a brief description of each of the places listed below. Ask other classmates for help if you need it.**

Locations		Information needed	
restaurant	bookstore	name	hours
public library	supermarket	address	description
park	your school	phone number	special events

F **Active Task:** Go to the Visitor's Bureau in your city or look on the Internet to find a Visitor's Guide for your city. What information does it have?

Review

A Imagine that you just moved into your neighborhood. Write four questions you might ask your new neighbor about different places to go. Then practice asking a partner those questions. Write down the suggestions your partner gives you.

Questions	Suggestions
1.	1.
2.	2.
3.	3.
4.	4.

B Now ask your partner to give you directions from the school to the four places he or she suggested. Write down the directions he or she gives you on a separate sheet of paper and double-check them with your partner.

C You are visiting the public library for the first time. Write three questions you might ask the librarian.

1. _____

2. _____

3. _____

Review

D **You have learned a lot in this unit about different places in the community that you can visit, volunteer, or do things at. Make a list of all the places in your community that you visit.**

Restaurants I eat at: _____

_____

Stores I shop at: _____

_____

Places that provide free services: _____

_____

Places I volunteer: _____

_____

Places my family and I go to school: _____

_____

Other: _____

_____

E **Now make a list of places you haven't been but would like to go.**

Restaurants _____

Stores _____

Places that provide free services _____

Places to volunteer _____

Places to go to school _____

Other _____

F **Make a list of ways you can get information about the places you listed above. (All of this information will help you with your team project.)**

1. _____

2. _____

3. _____

4. _____

Create a community pamphlet

With a team, you will create a community pamphlet or part of a pamphlet. This project can be done two ways:

1. Each team creates its own pamphlet.

2. Each team creates a portion of a pamphlet and all parts will be combined at the end.

1. Form a team with four or five students. Choose positions for each member of your team.

Position	Job Description	Student Name
Student 1 Leader	See that everyone speaks English. See that everyone participates.	
Student 2 Community Representative	Take notes and write information for pamphlet.	
Student 3 Artist	Design and add art to pamphlet.	
Students 4/5 Member(s)	Help community representative and designer with their work.	

2. As a class, decide what information should go in your pamphlet (For example: local services, medical facilities, restaurants, events). Make a list on the board.

3. Decide if each team will create its own pamphlet or if each team will work on a portion of the pamphlet. (If the second option is chosen, decide what section each team will work on.)

4. Create your pamphlet or portion of the pamphlet. Make sure to include addresses, phone numbers, and basic information. (Use the phone book or Internet if you need to.)

5. Put your pamphlet together.

6. Present your pamphlet or portion of your pamphlet to the class.

PRONUNCIATION

Word Linking. Listen to the sentences below and notice how the words *could, would,* and *did* are linked to the following word *you.* They sound like *kudju, wudju,* and *didju.* Listen again and repeat. Make new sentences to practice these sounds.

1. Could you tell me when the store opens?

2. Would you show me where the elevators are?

3. Did you find the phone number?

LEARNER LOG

In this unit, you learned many things about community. How comfortable do you feel doing each of the skills listed below? Rate your comfort level on a scale of 1 to 4.

1 = Not so comfortable **2** = Need more practice **3** = Comfortable **4** = Very comfortable

If you circle 1 or 2, write down the page number where you can review this skill.

Life Skill	Comfort Level				Page(s)
I can identify and ask for resources in a community.	1	2	3	4	_____
I can ask about resources in a community.	1	2	3	4	_____
I can identify recreational programs.	1	2	3	4	_____
I can read a community bulletin board.	1	2	3	4	_____
I can understand library resource information.	1	2	3	4	_____
I can identify and access library services.	1	2	3	4	_____
I can interpret a road map.	1	2	3	4	_____
I can give and receive directions using a road map.	1	2	3	4	_____
I can volunteer in my community.	1	2	3	4	_____
I can read and interpret location and event descriptions.	1	2	3	4	_____
I can create location descriptions.	1	2	3	4	_____

Grammar

	Comfort Level				Page(s)
I can use embedded questions to ask for information.	1	2	3	4	_____
I can make suggestions.	1	2	3	4	_____

Reflection

Complete the following statements with your thoughts from this unit.

I learned _____

I would like to find out more about _____

I am still confused about _____

UNIT
5

Health

GOALS

- Make a bar graph
- Use the present perfect continuous
- Use indirect speech

- Fill out a health insurance form
- Read for detail
- Interpret medicine labels
- Write a summary

LESSON

Health habits

GOAL ▶ Make a bar graph   *Academic skill*

A What are the following people doing? Which activities are healthy? Which activities are unhealthy? Make two lists below.

Healthy habits	Unhealthy habits

B Can you think of other healthy or unhealthy activities? Add a good and a bad habit to your list.

C Ms. Tracy's 25 students took a poll in their class to find out what bad health habits they have. They presented their results in the form of a bar graph. Read the bar graph and answer the questions.

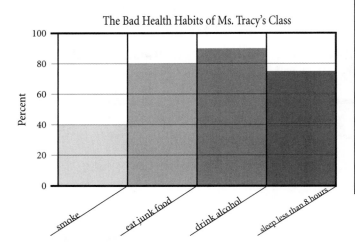

The Bad Health Habits of Ms. Tracy's Class

How to Calculate Percentage
1. First, find out the total number of students in your class.
2. Then divide the total number of students into the number of students who answered the question yes.
EXAMPLE: In a class of 25 students, 15 students exercise.
$$25\overline{)15.00}$$ with quotient .60, 15 00, 00
3. Move the decimal over two places to the right to get the percentage.
.60 = 60%

1. What percentage of students eat junk food? _____

2. What percentage of students sleep less than eight hours? _____

3. What percentage of students *don't* smoke? _____

4. What percentage of students *don't* drink alcohol? _____

5. What is the worst health habit Ms. Tracy's class shares? _____

D With a group of students, make a list of four good health habits and take a poll in your class. Make sure you ask every student in the class. Based on your findings, make a bar graph.

Example question: Do you exercise?

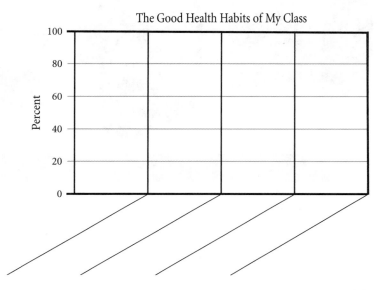

The Good Health Habits of My Class

E **Active Task:** Take a poll among your family and friends of the health habits in exercise D. Make a bar graph.

What's the problem?

GOAL ▶ Use the present perfect continuous   *Grammar*

Who are the people in
the picture?
What are they saying?

A Read the conversation between the doctor and patient.

Doctor: Hello, John. What seems to be the problem?
John: Well, <u>I've been coughing</u> a lot.
Doctor: Anything else?
John: Yes, <u>my chest has been hurting</u>, too.
Doctor: It sounds like you might have <u>bronchitis</u>. I'd like to do some tests to be sure, and then I'll give you a prescription to relieve your symptoms.
John: Thanks, Doc.

B Practice the conversation with a partner. Then practice the conversation again, replacing the underlined parts with the information below.

Symptom no. 1	Symptom no. 2	Diagnosis
1. I've been blowing my nose a lot.	My back has been aching.	a common cold
2. My leg's been hurting.	I haven't been walking properly.	a muscle spasm
3. I've been throwing up.	I've been feeling faint and dizzy.	the flu

C Study the chart with your teacher.

Present perfect continuous		
Example	**Form**	**When do you use it?**
I *have been studying* for three hours. The president *has been speaking* since 9 A.M.	*Affirmative sentence* *has/have + been +* present participle	To emphasize the duration of an activity or state that started in the past and continues in the present
You've *been going* to the movies a lot lately. He *hasn't been working* late recently.	*Negative sentence* *has/have + not + been +* present participle	To show that an activity has been in progress recently
How long *have they lived / been living* here? They *have lived / have been living* here since 2000.	*Question* *has/have +* subject *+ been +* present participle	With some verbs (*work, live, teach*), there is no difference in meaning between the present perfect and the present perfect continuous.

Note: Some verbs are not usually used in the continuous form, e.g., *be, believe, hate, have, know, like, want.*

D Complete the following sentences using the present perfect continuous and suitable time expressions.

for + period of time	*since* + point in time
two weeks five days a month a long time a while	Tuesday 5:30 P.M. 1964 last night I was a child

1. We _____ (study)

   English for _____ .

2. The kids _____ (sleep)

   since _____ .

3. The couple _____ (travel) in Mexico for _____ .

4. I _____ (work) at the same job for _____ .

5. How long _____ (you/teach) math?

6. Satomi _____ (feel well/not) since _____ .

7. The boy _____ (read) since _____ .

8. Enrico _____ (play piano) for _____ .

9. Minh _____ (think) about changing jobs for _____ .

10. _____ (they/live) in New York for _____ ?

E Now review the present perfect with your teacher.

Present perfect simple		
Example	**Form**	**When do you use it?**
He *has seen* the doctor. *Have* you *called* your mother? She *has* never *broken* her arm.	*Affirmative Sentence* has/have + past participle	When something happened (or didn't happen) at an unspecified time in the past
I *have moved* four times in my life. She *has been* to the hospital many times.	*Negative Sentence* has/have + not + past participle *or* has/have + never + past participle	When something happened more than once in the past (and could possibly happen again in the future)
They *have lived* here for ten years. I *have had* bronchitis since last week.	*Question* has/have + subject + past participle	When something started at a specific time in the past and continues in the present

F Choose the present perfect or the present perfect continuous to complete these sentences.

1. They _____ (be) to New York several times.

2. Marco _____ (have) three jobs since 1995.

3. She _____ (give) me a lot of help since I moved here.

4. I _____ (study) Spanish recently.

5. _____ (you/see) the Tower of Pisa in Italy?

6. _____ (you/wait) for a long time?

7. Santiago _____ (miss/not) any classes this week.

8. We _____ (live) here for three years.

9. John _____ (talk) to the doctor for 20 minutes.

10. How long _____ (you/know) Maria?

G Work in groups of three or four. Ask and answer questions using *How long . . . ?* Use the present perfect or present perfect continuous.

EXAMPLES:
How long have you been studying English?
How long have you been at this school?

What did she say?

GOAL ▶ Use indirect speech

> What are Rosa and her friend talking about? What do you think they are saying?

A **Listen to the following conversation between Rosa and her doctor. Number the sentences in the correct order.**

_____ "I can give you some more tests."

_____ "The most important thing is to stay active."

_____ "You have to come back in two weeks."

_____ "If you do more exercise, your cholesterol should go down."

_____ "If you don't stop eating junk food, you will have serious health problems."

B **Now listen to Rosa reporting her conversation to her friend. Fill in the missing words.**

1. The doctor said that she _____ give _____ some more tests.

2. The doctor told me that the most important thing _____ to stay active.

3. The doctor said that if _____ _____ stop eating junk food, _____ _____ have serious health problems.

4. The doctor told me that if _____ _____ more exercise, _____ cholesterol should go down.

5. The doctor said that _____ _____ _____ to come back in two weeks.

C **What differences do you notice between the sentences in exercise A and exercise B? Study the chart below with your teacher.**

Direct speech	Indirect speech	Rule
"You have to exercise more."	The doctor *told me* (that) I had to exercise more.	Change pronoun.
"The most important thing is to stay active."	The doctor *said* (that) the most important thing *was* to stay active.	Change present tense to past tense.

D Match the type of doctor with the treatment he or she provides.

| dentist | chiropractor | podiatrist | pediatrician | obstetrician |

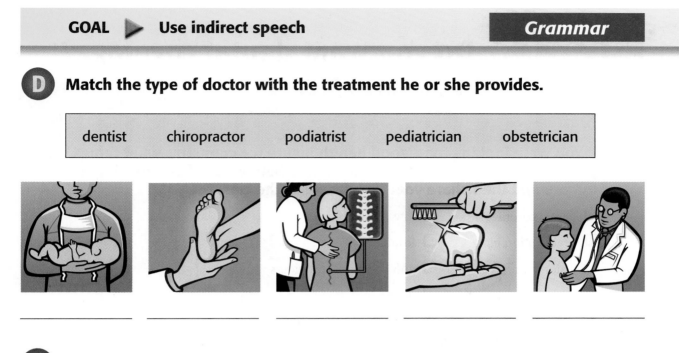

_____   _____   _____   _____   _____

E Read each statement below. Decide what type of doctor said each statement and use indirect speech to tell your partner what each person said. Then write the sentences below.

EXAMPLE:
"You are in perfect health!"
The doctor told me I was in perfect health.

1. "You need to brush your gums and floss your teeth every day."

_____

2. "Your children are eating too many sweets and sugary foods. They need to eat more fruits and vegetables."

_____

_____

3. "It is good idea to go to prenatal classes for at least three weeks."

_____

_____

4. "The shoes you are wearing aren't good for your feet."

_____

5. "You'll hurt your back if you don't bend your knees to lift heavy objects."

_____

_____

F **Active Task:** Think of a conversation you had recently with a friend, family member, co-worker, or your teacher. Tell your partner what the person said to you.

4 Do you want dental coverage?

GOAL ▶ Fill out a health insurance form   *Life skill*

A If you were looking for a good health insurance company, what things would you look for? Check ✓ which of the items below would be most important for you and then share your answers with the class.

❑ dental coverage   ❑ low deductible

❑ prescription plan   ❑ low co-pay

❑ vision plan   ❑ good choice of providers

❑ low premium   ❑ good reputation

B Skim the health insurance application on this page and the next page. Put a check ✓ next to every part you can answer. Underline parts you are not sure about.

Employee Applicant Information:

First Name: _____   Middle Name: _____   Last Name: _____

Home Address: Street: _____   City: _____   State:_____   Zip Code: _____

Sex: ____ Male ____ Female

Social Security Number: _____

Date of birth: (mm/dd/yyyy) _____

Marital Status: ____ Married ____ Single

Work Phone: _____   Home Phone:_____

Job Title: _____

Hours Worked per Week: _____   Annual Salary: _____

Tobacco: Have you or your spouse used any tobacco products in the past 12 months?

Employee: ____ Yes ____ No

Spouse: ____ Yes ____ No

Dental: Do you want Dental Coverage? ____ Yes ____ No

Prescription Card: Do you want a Prescription Card? ____ Yes ____ No

Dependents: Dependents you want covered on this policy.

Spouse: _____

Date of birth: (mm/dd/yyyy) _____ Sex: ____ Male ____ Female

Child #1: _____

Date of birth: (mm/dd/yyyy) _____ Sex: ____ Male ____ Female

Child #2: _____

Date of birth: (mm/dd/yyyy) _____ Sex: ____ Male ____ Female

A-1: Within the last four (4) years, have you or any dependent received or been recommended to have treatment for any disorders or conditions of the following? Please check all that apply.

❑ Back	❑ Stroke	❑ Intestinal	❑ Colon
❑ Kidney	❑ Muscular	❑ Heart or Circulatory	❑ Cancer
❑ Diabetes	❑ Respiratory	❑ Mental or Emotional	❑ Liver

A-2: Within the last four (4) years, have you or any dependent used drugs not prescribed by a physician, been advised to have treatment or been treated for drug abuse or alcoholism, or been a member of Alcoholics Anonymous?
❑ Yes ❑ No

A-3: Have you or any dependent ever had a positive blood test indicating HIV antibodies or been treated and/or advised by a medical practitioner as having Acquired Immune Deficiency Syndrome (AIDS), AIDS Related Complex (ARC), or any other immune system deficiency?
❑ Yes ❑ No

A-4: Have you or any dependent been hospitalized, had surgery, or had more than $5000 in medical expenses in the last twelve (12) months?
❑ Yes ❑ No

A-5: Are you or any dependent pregnant? ❑ Yes ❑ No
If "Yes," what is your estimated due date? _____

A-6: Within the last four (4) years, have you or any dependent received or been recommended to have treatment for any disorders or conditions of the following? Please check all that apply.

❑ Ear	❑ Hernia	❑ Thyroid	❑ Breast
❑ Eye	❑ Allergy	❑ Digestive System	❑ Joint
❑ Asthma	❑ Reproductive Organs	❑ Ulcer	❑ Arthritis
❑ High Blood Pressure			

A-7: Within the last four (4) years, have you or any dependent received treatment or been advised to seek treatment for any reason not already mentioned?
❑ Yes ❑ No

Employee Name: _____

Date: (mm/dd/yyyy) _____

C **Work in pairs and use a dictionary to help you understand the parts of the form that you underlined.**

D **Why do you think health insurance companies need this information? Why is it important to have health insurance?**

E **Active Task:** Find a health insurance application form from a health insurance company or from the Internet. Fill out the application. (Don't send it in unless you're sure you want to get health insurance through them!)

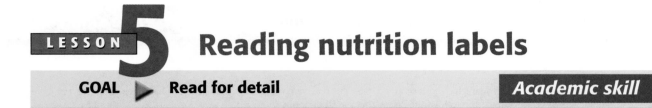

A Do you always read the nutrition label on food that you buy? What do you usually read first on the label? Why?

B Look at the nutrition label below. Answer the questions.

1. How many calories are in one serving of this product? How many of those calories are from fat?
2. How much protein is in this product?
3. What vitamins or minerals does this product contain?
4. How many carbohydrates are in one serving of this product?
5. How much fat is in one serving of this product? How much of the fat is saturated?
6. What is one serving of this product?

Nutrition Facts
Serving Size 2oz. (56gm)
Servings Per Container 8

Amount Per Serving

Calories 200	Calories from Fat 10

	% Daily Value*
Total Fat 1g	2%
Saturated Fat 0g	
Cholesterol 0mg	
Sodium 0mg	
Total Carbohydrate 42g	14%
Dietary Fiber 2g	8%
Sugars 1g	
Protein 7g	
Vitamin A	0%
Calcium	0%
Thiamin	35%
Niacin	15%
Vitamin C	0%
Iron	10%
Riboflavin	15%
Folate	30%

*Percent Daily Values are based on a 2,000 calorie diet. Your daily values may be higher or lower depending on your calorie needs:

Calories	2,000	2,500
Total Fat	Less than 65g	80g
Sat Fat	Less than 20g	25g
Cholesterol	Less than 300mg	300mg
Sodium	Less than 2,400mg	2,400mg
Total Carbohydrate	300g	375g
Dietary Fiber	25g	30g

Calories per gram:
Fat 9   Carbohydrate 4   Protein 4

INGREDIENTS: SEMOLINA, NIACIN, IRON, THIAMIN MONONITRATE, RIBOFLAVIN, FOLIC ACID.

C Match the highlighted words from the label with the definitions below.

1. This is the amount of food that a person actually eats at one time. _____

2. This type of nutrient indicates the salt content of food. _____

3. This ingredient of food is not digested, but it aids digestion. _____

4. These indicate the total amount of energy supplied by a kind of food. _____

5. This helps to build and repair muscles. It is found mainly in meat, fish, eggs, beans, and cheese. _____

6. These are whatever is contained in a type of food. _____

7. This is a type of fat. It can contribute to heart disease. _____

8. This is the best source of energy and can be found in breads, grains, fruits, and vegetables. _____

9. Eating too much of this can cause heart disease. _____

10. These nutrients help to keep your body healthy. _____

D **Read the following information about food labels.**

Reading Nutritional Information on Food Labels

Knowing how to read the food label on packaged foods can help you build better eating habits. Here's a rundown of the basics you'll find on a food label and how you can use the information to improve your daily diet:

1. **Serving Size** The serving sizes on the label are supposed to be close to "real life" serving sizes - no more listing a teaspoon of dressing when most of us use a tablespoon. The information on the rest of the label is based on data for one serving. Remember, a package may contain more than one serving.

2. **Calories** The number of calories tells you how many calories are in one serving. The number of calories from fat tells you how many calories come from fat. Try to find foods with low amounts of calories from fat.

3. **Fat** This is where you look if you are trying to count fat grams. Total fat is important to watch, but saturated fat is particularly bad for you. Saturated fat raises your blood cholesterol level and that could lead to heart troubles.

4. **Cholesterol** Along with saturated fat, cholesterol amounts are important for anyone concerned about heart disease. High levels of cholesterol can lead to serious heart problems later in life.

5. **Sodium** Sodium (or salt) levels are important to monitor if you have high blood pressure.

6. **Carbohydrates** These fit into two categories: complex carbohydrates (dietary fiber) and simple carbohydrates (sugars). Diets high in complex carbohydrates have been shown to fight cancer and heart disease. Simple carbohydrates are good for energy, but eat too much of them and you can expect your waistline to grow.

7. **Fiber** Fiber consists of complex carbohydrates that cannot be absorbed by the body. It aids digestion and can help to lower blood cholesterol. High fiber foods include fruits, vegetables, brown rice, and whole grain products.

8. **Protein** The food label doesn't specify a daily percentage or guideline for protein consumption because so much depends on individual needs. An athlete needs more than an office worker, but in a typical 2,000-calorie diet, most people need no more than 50 grams of protein per day.

9. **Vitamins and Minerals** The FDA requires only Vitamin A, Vitamin C, Iron, and Calcium on this label, although food companies can voluntarily list others. The FDA feels these four vitamins and minerals are particularly important in order to maintain a healthy diet. Try and get 100 percent of each every day.

10. **Ingredients** These are listed on a food label by weight from the most to the least. This section can alert you to any ingredients you may want to avoid because of food allergies.

E **How much do you know about nutrition? Fill in the circle under *True* or *False* for each statement below.**

	True	False
1. Reading food labels can help to improve your eating habits.	○	○
2. Diets high in complex carbohydrates can help to fight cancer and heart disease.	○	○
3. Saturated fat lowers your blood cholesterol level.	○	○
4. You should watch your sodium intake if you have high blood pressure.	○	○
5. Most people need at least 100 grams of protein per day.	○	○
6. Simple carbohydrates are good for energy.	○	○
7. Foods with fiber can help to lower cholesterol.	○	○

F **Active Task:** Read the food labels of your favorite products or look them up on the Internet. Share the information with your class.

Take two aspirin

GOAL ▶ Interpret medicine labels

Life skill

A Identify the medicines in the pictures below. Are they usually prescription or non-prescription? What illnesses or conditions are they used for?

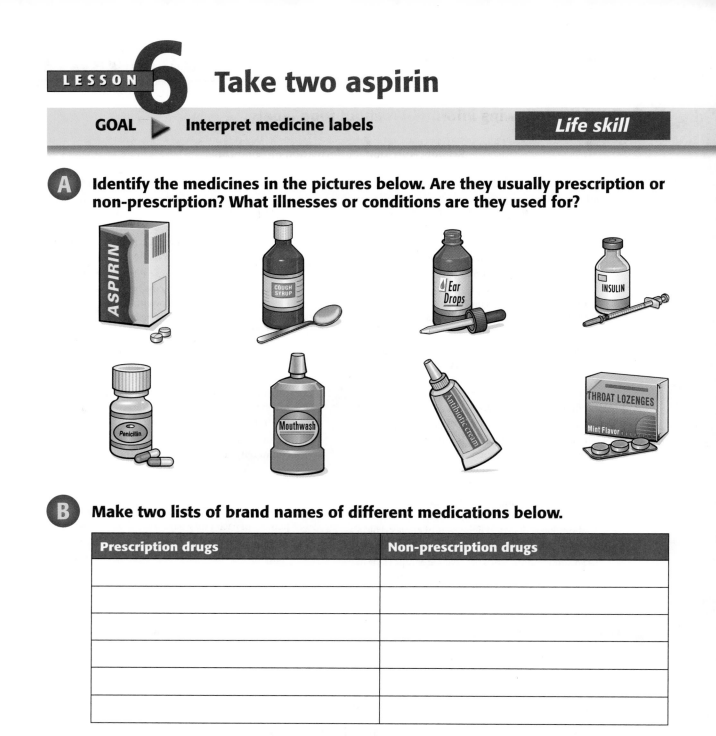

B Make two lists of brand names of different medications below.

Prescription drugs	Non-prescription drugs

C Now look at each drug on your lists. What is each one used for? Why is each one prescription or non-prescription? Discuss it with your group and then share your answers with the class.

D **Active Task:** Find out at the library or on the Internet which of the following drugs are prescription and which are non-prescription. What are they used for?

aspirin	penicillin	antihistamine	ibuprofen	codeine	valium

E Below is a list of phrases you might find on a medicine label. Decide if each phrase is an indication, a direction, or a warning. Fill in the circle under the correct answer.

	Indication	Direction	Warning
1. Do not exceed two doses in any 24-hour period. Use only as directed.	○	○	○
2. Temporarily relieves common cold/flu symptoms.	○	○	○
3. Take two tablespoons in dose cup provided.	○	○	○
4. For the temporary relief of minor aches and pains.	○	○	○
5. Adults: Take one tablet every 4 to 6 hours.	○	○	○
6. In case of accidental overdose, contact a poison control center immediately.	○	○	○

F Read the medicine labels and answer the questions below.

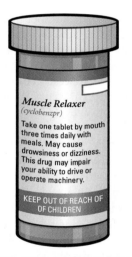

Muscle Relaxer
(cyclobenzpr)
Take one tablet by mouth three times daily with meals. May cause drowsiness or dizziness. This drug may impair your ability to drive or operate machinery.

KEEP OUT OF REACH OF CHILDREN

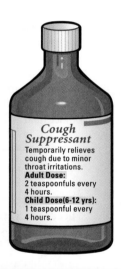

Cough Suppressant
Temporarily relieves cough due to minor throat irritations.
Adult Dose:
2 teaspoonfuls every 4 hours.
Child Dose(6-12 yrs):
1 teaspoonful every 4 hours.

	Muscle relaxer	Cough suppressant
1. How often can you take this medicine?		
2. Can you drive a car or operate machinery while taking this drug?		
3. Do you have to take this drug with food?		
4. Can children take this medicine?		
5. What symptoms will this drug relieve?		

G **Active Task:** At home or on the Internet, look at the labels of drugs that you or your family members take. Answer the questions above for each drug.

LESSON 7 — The common cold

GOAL ▶ **Write a summary**

Academic skill

A **What do you know about the common cold? Discuss each of the topics below.**

Does Vitamin C Have a Role?   How Can We Prevent Colds?   What Are Cold Symptoms?
What Is the Treatment?   The Problem   How Do Colds Spread?

B **Read the article and write the correct heading for each paragraph.**

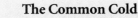

The Common Cold

_____

In the course of a year, individuals in the United States suffer 1 billion colds, according to some estimates. Children have about six to ten colds a year. In families with children in school, the number of colds per child can be as high as 12 a year. Adults average about two to four colds a year. Women, especially those aged 20 to 30 years, have more colds than men, possibly because of their closer contact with children. On average, individuals older than 60 have less than one cold a year.

_____

Symptoms of the common cold usually begin two to three days after infection and often include sneezing, sore throat, cough, and headache. Fever is usually slight but can climb to 102 degrees Fahrenheit in infants and young children. Cold symptoms can last from two to fourteen days, but two-thirds of people recover in a week. If symptoms occur often or last much longer than two weeks, they may be the result of an allergy rather than a cold.

_____

Depending on the virus type, any or all of the following routes of transmission may be common:
• Touching infectious respiratory secretions on skin and on environmental surfaces and then touching the eyes or nose.
• Inhaling relatively large particles of respiratory secretions transported briefly in the air.

• Inhaling droplet nuclei: smaller infectious particles suspended in the air for long periods of time.

_____

Hand-washing is the simplest and most effective way to keep from getting rhinovirus colds. Not touching the nose or eyes is another. Individuals with colds should always sneeze or cough into a facial tissue and promptly throw it away. If possible, one should avoid close, prolonged exposure to persons who have colds. Cleaning environmental surfaces with a virus-killing disinfectant might help prevent spread of infection.

_____

Only symptomatic treatment is available for uncomplicated cases of the common cold: bed rest, plenty of fluids, gargling with warm salt water, petroleum jelly for a raw nose, and aspirin or acetaminophen to relieve headache or fever.

_____

Many people are convinced that taking large quantities of vitamin C will prevent colds or relieve symptoms. To test this theory, several large-scale, controlled studies involving children and adults have been conducted. To date, no conclusive data has shown that large doses of vitamin C prevent colds.

Source: The National Institute of Allergy and Infectious Diseases of The National Institutes of Health. Fact Sheet: **The Common Cold**. June 1996. Last revised May 1998. (Online) http://www.niaid.nih.gov/factsheets/cold.htm

C What is the title and source of the article?

_____

D Summarize the main topic of the article in one sentence.

The article describes _____

_____

E Write one sentence to summarize each paragraph by completing the sentences below.

Paragraph 1: Colds are a problem because _____

_____

Paragraph 2: The symptoms include _____

_____

Paragraph 3: Colds are spread by _____

Paragraph 4: Some ways of preventing colds are _____

_____

Paragraph 5: Some ways of treating a cold are _____

_____

Paragraph 6: Vitamin C _____

_____

F Rewrite two of the sentences from exercise E starting with *The author states that . . .* or *The article says that . . . .*

1. _____

_____

2. _____

_____

G What is a summary? Why do we write summaries? Why are they useful? Discuss as a class.

H **When you write a summary, follow these rules.**

Rules for writing a summary

1. Read the article carefully.

2. Make a brief outline.

    I. Main idea

        A. Important supporting point

        B. Important supporting point

        C. Important supporting point

3. Identify the main idea and write it first.

4. Identify only the most important supporting points, and omit unnecessary details.

5. Don't repeat ideas.

6. Don't change the author's meaning.

7. Use your own words, but don't include your own ideas or comments.

8. Mention the source of the selection and the author at the beginning.

9. Present the ideas in the order in which they were discussed in the article.

10. Remind the reader that you are summarizing someone else's ideas by using citation expressions. (See box.)

How to cite sources in summaries

The author . . .

says that	emphasizes that
states that	argues that
explains that	maintains that
points out that	highlights the fact that
mentions that	concludes that

I **Follow the rules above and use your answers from page 95 to write a summary of the article on a separate sheet of paper.**

J **Active Task:** Find an interesting article in the newspaper or on the Internet. Write a summary using the guidelines above.

Review

A What are three good health habits discussed in this unit?

1. _____
2. _____
3. _____

B What are three bad health habits discussed in this unit?

1. _____
2. _____
3. _____

C Complete these sentences using the present perfect or present perfect continuous.

1. I (not / eat) _____ meat for three years.

2. Sara (go) _____ to yoga classes since September.

3. Andres (drink) _____ two liters of water today.

4. I (not / sleep) _____ well recently.

5. I (never / smoke) _____ a cigarette.

6. Why (you / choose) _____ such a stressful job?

D Change the following sentences from direct speech to indirect speech.

1. "My daughter is sick."

   Maria said _____

2. "We won't be able to come to the meeting."

   Luis and Ricardo told me _____

3. "You have to take two pills every day."

   The doctor told me _____

4. "Your son is eating too much sugar."

   The pediatrician said _____

5. "My back has been hurting for two months."

   I told the chiropractor _____

E Make a list of ten new vocabulary words you used this unit.

1. _____   6. _____

2. _____   7. _____

3. _____   8. _____

4. _____   9. _____

5. _____   10. _____

F Make word families for four of the words from your list.

Noun	Verb	Adjective	Adverb
1.			
2.			
3.			
4.			

G Find words in this unit to complete the following sentences. The answers are all names of different kinds of food nutrients.

1. _____ indicates the amount of salt content in your food.

2. _____ are the amount of energy supplied by a kind of food.

3. _____ helps to build and repair muscles.

4. _____ fat is a type of fat that causes heart disease.

H Complete the sentences below. Share your answers with a group of students and choose the best answer in the group. Report your answers to the class.

1. We need health insurance forms when we _____

_____

2. We need to read nutrition labels if we want to _____

_____

3. It is important to understand medicine labels because _____

_____

4. It is useful to write summaries because _____

_____

Create a community health pamphlet

With a team, you will create a pamphlet to distribute to the community about good health practices.

1. Form a team with four or five students. Choose positions for each member of your team.

Position	Job Description	Student Name
Student 1 Leader	See that everyone speaks English. See that everyone participates.	
Student 2 Secretary	Take notes and write information for pamphlet.	
Student 3 Designer	Design and add art to pamphlet.	
Students 4/5 Member (s)	Help secretary and designer with their work.	

2. With your team, decide what information should go in your pamphlet. (Ideas: good health habits, nutrition, reading medicine labels, etc.)

3. Write the text and decide on the art to use in your pamphlet.

4. Put your pamphlet together.

5. Present your pamphlet to the class.

PRONUNCIATION

Word Linking. In spoken English, the pronoun *he* often loses its initial /h/ sound when it is linked to the previous word. Listen and repeat.

1. Is he taking any medication? (*izzy*)
2. Has he been ill for a long time? (*hazzy*)
3. Does he often go to the doctor? (*duzzy*)
4. Did he give you some advice? (*diddy*)
5. Isn't he going to take sick leave? (*izzeny*)
6. Hasn't he phoned yet? (*hazzeny*)
7. Doesn't he have insurance? (*duzzeny*)
8. Didn't he tell you about the pills? (*diddeny*)

LEARNER LOG

In this unit, you learned many things about health. How comfortable do you feel doing each of the skills listed below? Rate your comfort level on a scale of 1 to 4.

1 = Not so comfortable **2** = Need more practice **3** = Comfortable **4** = Very comfortable

If you circle 1 or 2, write down the page number where you can review this skill.

Life Skill	Comfort Level	Page(s)
I can identify good and bad health habits.	1 2 3 4	_____
I can report illness and symptoms.	1 2 3 4	_____
I can interpret and fill out health insurance forms.	1 2 3 4	_____
I can identify vitamins and nutritional content of foods.	1 2 3 4	_____
I can interpret nutritional information.	1 2 3 4	_____
I can identify prescription and non-prescription drugs.	1 2 3 4	_____
I can interpret instructions on medicine labels.	1 2 3 4	_____

Grammar		
I can use the present perfect and the present perfect continuous.	1 2 3 4	_____
I can use indirect speech to report a conversation with the doctor.	1 2 3 4	_____

Academic Skill		
I can interpret information about the common cold.	1 2 3 4	_____
I can write a summary.	1 2 3 4	_____

Reflection

Complete the following statements with your thoughts about this unit.

I learned _____

I would like to find out more about _____

I am still confused about _____

Getting Hired

GOALS

- Complete a skills inventory
- Use adjective clauses
- Conduct a job search
- Use the past perfect
- Write a resume
- Write a cover letter
- Prepare for a job interview

What skills do you have?

GOAL ▶ Complete a skills inventory　　　*Vocabulary*

A Read the list of characteristics that employers look for in good employees. Which ones describe you? Discuss each of them with your class and check the ones that apply to you.

❏ dependable	❏ hard-working	❏ responsible
❏ detail-oriented	❏ open-minded	❏ self-motivated
❏ efficient	❏ patient	❏ a team player
❏ flexible	❏ a problem solver	❏ well-organized
❏ good with numbers	❏ a quick learner	❏ willing to accept responsibility
❏ great with people	❏ reliable	❏ works well under pressure

B Are there other personal skills or qualities that aren't listed above?

_____　　　_____

_____　　　_____

_____　　　_____

_____　　　_____

C Why is each of the above skills important? Discuss what jobs might be good for a person with each skill.

D **Match the sentences below with words from exercise A.**

1. Suzanne works long hours and never takes any breaks. _____

2. You can always count on Linh. _____

3. Tran isn't afraid of making decisions. _____

4. Li is always calm, even when it's very stressful. _____

5. You never have to explain anything to Vlasta twice. _____

6. Chan can always find any file immediately. _____

7. Arnold takes time to explain everything carefully to every customer. _____

8. Let's ask Phuong. She's good at thinking of different solutions. _____

E **Listen to four people describe their skills and interests. Take notes in the first column. Then suggest a job for each of them in the second column.**

Lam	Skills and interests	Most suitable job
Lilia		
Morteza		
Hilda		

F **List your skills and interests. What are some jobs that you think you might enjoy and be good at? On a separate piece of paper, make a list of three jobs and three skills.**

G **Active Task:** Ask your family and friends what they think your best skills are.

LESSON 2

What does an accountant do?

| GOAL ▷ | Use adjective clauses | *Grammar* |

A Look at the pictures. What jobs are the people doing? Discuss with a partner.

B Below is a list of job titles and responsibilities. Work in groups of three and ask each other questions to complete the missing information. Then add two of your own job titles to the list.

Job title	Job responsibilities
accountant	_____
administrative assistant	_____
assembler	_____
cashier	_____
computer technician	*repairs computers* ____
delivery person	_____
dental assistant	_____
garment worker	_____
gas station attendant	_____
hairdresser	*cuts hair* _____
homemaker	_____
lawyer	_____
police officer	_____
postal worker	_____
receptionist	_____
salesperson	_____
security guard	_____
_____	_____
_____	_____

C From the list above, choose three jobs that you would like to have. What skills do you have that would be necessary for each of these jobs?

D **Study the chart with your teacher.**

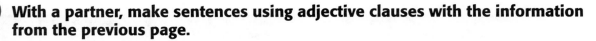

Adjective clauses		
Restrictive adjective clauses	A homemaker is a person *who maintains a home and a family.* I applied for the job *which was in the paper on Sunday.*	*Restrictive adjective clauses* give essential information about the noun they refer to. They cannot be omitted without losing the meaning of the sentence. They do not need commas.
Non-restrictive adjective clauses	My brother-in-law, *who owns his own business,* works very hard. I quit my job, *which I never really liked anyway.*	*Non-restrictive adjective clauses* give extra non-essential information about the noun they refer to. They can be omitted. They need commas.

E **With a partner, make sentences using adjective clauses with the information from the previous page.**

EXAMPLE:
Student A: A person who takes care of the home and the family is a _____.
Student B: Homemaker.

F **Look at exercise F on page 102 where you wrote three job titles and your skills for each of those jobs. Make sentences about your partner using non-restrictive adjective clauses.**

Job title	Skills	Sentence
Ex. *car salesperson*	*likes talking to people, knows a lot about cars*	*Aaron, who likes talking to people and knows a lot about cars, would make a great car salesman.*

 G **Write down two sentences about your job (or a job you would like to have). Give the sentences to your partner to combine into one sentence using an adjective clause.**

Sentence 1: _____

Sentence 2: _____

Combined sentence: _____

 Active Task: Talk to three different people about their jobs. Ask them what their job title is and what their responsibilities are.

LESSON 3 Looking for a job

| GOAL ▶ Conduct a job search | *Life skill* |

A **What is the best way to look for a job?**

_____

_____

_____

B **What are some things you need to think about before you begin your job search? Make a list.**

EXAMPLE: ***What hours can I work?***

1. _____   3. _____

2. _____   4. _____

5. _____

C **When you find a job opportunity, what information should you find out? Discuss the meaning of each of the following.**

- job title
- hours
- duties
- contact
- qualifications
- phone
- job location
- salary

D **Think about the job you have now. (Some of you may be students or homemakers. This is your job. If you are retired, think about your last job.) Fill in the chart below with information about your job.**

Information about your job	
Job title	
Job location	
Job duties	
Qualifications	
Hours	
Salary	

E **Active Task:** Look in the paper or on the Internet for a job that interests you and find out as much of the above information as you can. Share your findings with the class.

F Imagine you want to work for a company. It is important to find out some information about the company or business that you might work for. Fill in the chart below with your own ideas.

What kind of information is useful?	Where can you find this information?
Ex. *How many employees work for the company?*	*in the company brochure or on the Internet*
1.	1.
2.	2.
3.	3.
4.	4.
5.	5.

G Think about the company or business you work for now. Tell your partner about it. Make sure your partner is prepared to share this new information with the class.

H **Active Task:** Think of a company or business you have heard of and do some research on it. Find information in the library or on the Internet. Share your findings with the class.

My job, then and now

GOAL ▶ **Use the past perfect**   *Grammar*

A **Read about Ranjit.**

Ranjit Ghosh is from south India. He moved to the United States seven years ago. In India, he attended the National Computer School and received a certificate in computer repair. His first job was troubleshooting computer repairs for a financial company. After he moved to the United States, he started assembling computers and was able to use the skills he had learned during his course. Although he loves his job now, he needed another job to pay the bills. In addition to assembling, he also repairs computers in the evenings for another company. Ranjit is busy, but he is doing what he loves.

B **Answer the following questions about Ranjit.**

1. Ranjit has had three jobs. List them below with the most recent first.

   a. _____

   b. _____

   c. _____

2. Where did he go to school and what did he receive? _____

   _____

3. Why does Ranjit have two jobs in the United States? _____

   _____

C **Think about your own job history. Make a list of jobs below starting with the most recent first.**

Job History	
1. _____	4. _____
2. _____	5. _____
3. _____	6. _____

D Read the two sentences below. In each sentence, there are two things that happened. Which happened first? Write *first* or *second* under each idea.

Ranjit had attended school in India before he came to the United States.

_____   _____

Before Ranjit was hired to assemble computers, he had worked in computer repair.

_____   _____

Past perfect and simple past		
Example	**Form**	**Rule**
Before Ranjit moved to the United States, he *had lived* in India. = First he lived in India (past perfect) and then he moved to the United States. (simple past)	*had* + past participle	When describing two events that happened in the past, use the *past perfect* for the event that happened first.

E Combine the sentences below into one sentence using the past perfect for the event that happened first.

EXAMPLE:
(first) Santiago studied to be a teacher.
(second) Santiago was hired by the school district.

Santiago had studied to become a teacher before he was hired by the school district. *or*
After Santiago had studied to become a teacher, he was hired by the school district.

(first) Carolina worked as a cashier.
(second) Carolina became a food server.

_____

(first) Benjamin got his high school diploma.
(second) Benjamin enrolled in college classes.

_____

(first) Sandeep made money working for someone else.
(second) Sandeep opened his own dry cleaning business.

_____

F Look back to exercise C where you wrote your personal job history. On a separate piece of paper, write two sentences using the past perfect. Read your sentences aloud to the class.

Resumes

GOAL ▶ **Write a resume**

A   Read Ranjit's resume.

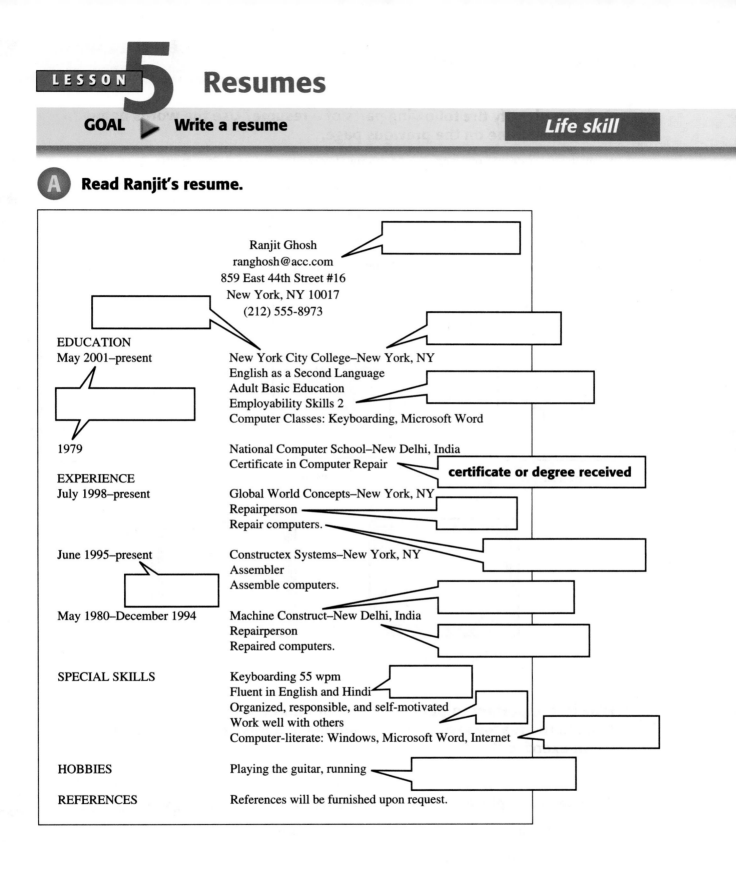

Ranjit Ghosh
ranghosh@acc.com
859 East 44th Street #16
New York, NY 10017
(212) 555-8973

EDUCATION
May 2001–present   New York City College–New York, NY
                        English as a Second Language
                        Adult Basic Education
                        Employability Skills 2
                        Computer Classes: Keyboarding, Microsoft Word

1979   National Computer School–New Delhi, India
                        Certificate in Computer Repair   **certificate or degree received**

EXPERIENCE
July 1998–present   Global World Concepts–New York, NY
                        Repairperson
                        Repair computers.

June 1995–present   Constructex Systems–New York, NY
                        Assembler
                        Assemble computers.

May 1980–December 1994 Machine Construct–New Delhi, India
                        Repairperson
                        Repaired computers.

SPECIAL SKILLS   Keyboarding 55 wpm
                        Fluent in English and Hindi
                        Organized, responsible, and self-motivated
                        Work well with others
                        Computer-literate: Windows, Microsoft Word, Internet

HOBBIES   Playing the guitar, running

REFERENCES   References will be furnished upon request.

B Can you identify the following parts of a resume? Use the words below to label the resume on the previous page.

- certificate or degree received
- dates of job
- computer skills
- dates of education
- job responsibilities

- name of company
- location of company
- names of classes taken
- skills
- name of school

- job title
- location of school
- languages
- things you enjoy doing
- name and address

transcript

letter of recommendation

resume

degree certificate

award

C Why is it important to put each piece of information on your resume? Discuss the reasons with a group and make notes next to each item on the list in exercise B.

D On a separate piece of paper, make a list of the following things: *(Answers will vary.)*

1. schools you have attended
2. classes you have taken
3. certificates or degrees you have received
4. awards you have received

5. names and locations of companies you have you worked for
6. job titles and responsibilities you have had
7. special skills you have (see page 101)
8. things you enjoy doing

E **Using the information you wrote for task D, write your resume on the lines below.**

_____(name)

_____

_____

_____

_____

EDUCATION

_____   _____

_____

_____   _____

EXPERIENCE

_____   _____

_____

_____   _____

_____

SPECIAL SKILLS   _____

_____

_____

HOBBIES   _____

REFERENCES   _____

_____

 F **Active Task:** Go to the library or use the Internet to find tips on how to write your resume. Type your resume.

GOAL ▶ **Write a cover letter**   *Life skill*

A   **Read the cover letter that Ranjit wrote to send with his resume. What is the purpose of a cover letter?**

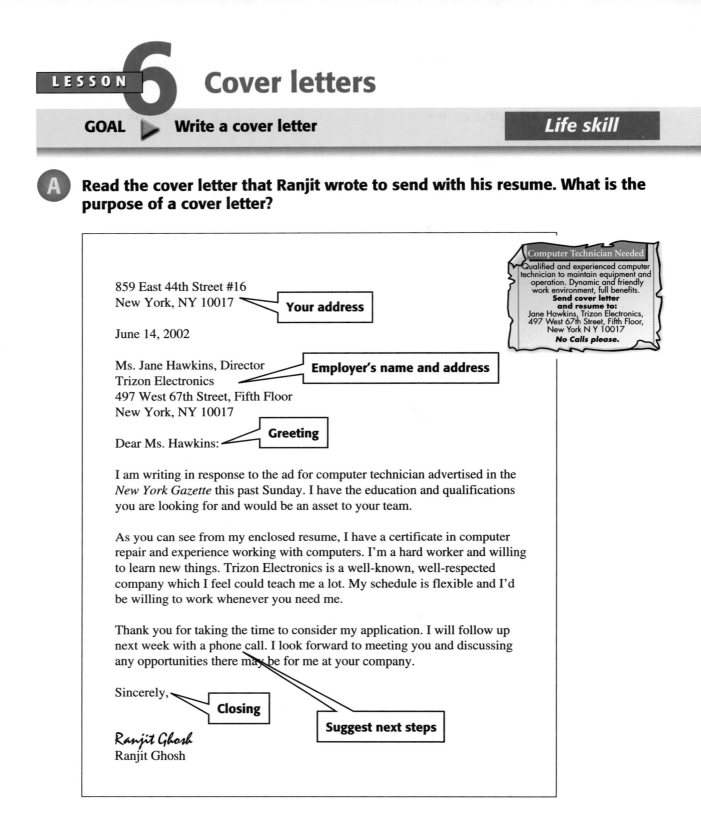

859 East 44th Street #16
New York, NY 10017   → **Your address**

June 14, 2002

Ms. Jane Hawkins, Director   → **Employer's name and address**
Trizon Electronics
497 West 67th Street, Fifth Floor
New York, NY 10017

Dear Ms. Hawkins: ← **Greeting**

I am writing in response to the ad for computer technician advertised in the *New York Gazette* this past Sunday. I have the education and qualifications you are looking for and would be an asset to your team.

As you can see from my enclosed resume, I have a certificate in computer repair and experience working with computers. I'm a hard worker and willing to learn new things. Trizon Electronics is a well-known, well-respected company which I feel could teach me a lot. My schedule is flexible and I'd be willing to work whenever you need me.

Thank you for taking the time to consider my application. I will follow up next week with a phone call. I look forward to meeting you and discussing any opportunities there may be for me at your company.

Sincerely,   → **Closing**

Suggest next steps

Ranjit Ghosh
Ranjit Ghosh

Ad box:
Computer Technician Needed
Qualified and experienced computer technician to maintain equipment and operation. Dynamic and friendly work environment, full benefits.
Send cover letter and resume to:
Jane Hawkins, Trizon Electronics, 497 West 67th Street, Fifth Floor, New York N Y 10017
No Calls please.

B **Read the following job descriptions. Choose one of the jobs that you would like to apply for.**

Work Solutions Inc.

Company Name: Healthy Living (61835 Valley Road, Grand Rapids, MI 49504)
Company Description: A company that produces and sells vitamins
Job Title: Warehouse Supervisor
Job Description: In charge of packaging orders in the warehouse. Must be able to supervise 20 employees. No experience with vitamins necessary, but warehouse experience would be helpful.

Company Name: Medical Valley Hospital (875 Washington Ave., Portland, OR 79468)
Job Title: Nurse's Aide
Job Description: Help the RNs take care of the patients. Fill out basic paperwork regarding patients, be able to take vital signs. No experience necessary—will train. Looking for someone who is friendly, patient, and likes working with sick people.

Company Name: Auto Land (75436 Harbor Blvd., Costa Mesa, CA 92627)
Company Description: Used car company
Job Title: Salesperson
Job Description: Selling cars. Must be good with people and outgoing. No sales experience necessary.

Company Name: Choicemart (876 San Miguel Street, Houston, TX 77042)
Job Title: Customer Service Representative
Job Description: Handle customer complaints, help customers fill out proper paperwork to file complaint, enter the complaint information into the computer, and set up meetings to discuss the complaints with the proper department. Must have good oral and written communication skills. Must be good with people and have the ability to handle angry customers. Basic computer skills helpful.

Company Name: Villa Italia (756 Fifth Ave., New York, NY 10019)
Job Title: Food Server
Job Description: Serve food to customers. Must have restaurant experience, but serving experience not necessary. Will train.

C **On a separate sheet of paper, write a cover letter to apply for one of the jobs above. Follow the model on page 112.**

GOAL ▶ **Prepare for a job interview**

A **Now that you have written your resume and your cover letter, it's time to get ready for the big interview! The best way to prepare for an interview is to practice.**

First, look at some sample interview questions. How would you answer each of them? Discuss each question with your group and then write out your answers on a separate piece of paper.

1. Tell me about yourself.

2. Why are you applying for this job?

3. Why do you think you would be good at this job?

4. What is your greatest strength?

5. What is your greatest weakness?

6. Do you prefer to work alone or with other people?

7. Why did you leave your last job?

8. What did you do at your last job?

9. Describe a situation where you had a conflict with another employee. How did you resolve it?

10. What special skills do you have that would benefit our company?

11. What is your present salary?

12. What did you like most about your last job?

13. Do you have any questions?
   (Answers will vary.)

B **With a partner, practice asking and answering the interview questions. It is OK to look at the answers you wrote for now.**

C In addition to your answers, job interviewers are also looking for other qualities. Read the list below. How would you rate on each of the qualities?

Handshake	○ Fair	○ Good	○ Excellent
Clothing	○ Fair	○ Good	○ Excellent
Eye contact with interviewer	○ Fair	○ Good	○ Excellent
Voice level (volume)	○ Fair	○ Good	○ Excellent
Facial expressions	○ Fair	○ Good	○ Excellent
Posture / body position	○ Fair	○ Good	○ Excellent
Self-confidence / comfort level	○ Fair	○ Good	○ Excellent
Willingness to volunteer information	○ Fair	○ Good	○ Excellent
Appropriateness of responses to questions	○ Fair	○ Good	○ Excellent
Ability to self-evaluate	○ Fair	○ Good	○ Excellent

D Looking at the list above, which two are you best at?

1. _____

2. _____

E Which two do you need to work on the most?

1. _____

2. _____

F Now it's time to practice. You will be interviewing for the job that you wrote your cover letter for. Work with a partner. Then switch roles.

Student A: Interviewer

Ask your partner at least ten of the questions on page 114. When the interview is over, fill out the Mock Interview Evaluation Form sheet on the next page in your partner's book.

Student B: Interviewee

Do your best to answer the questions without looking at your notes and try to rate highly on each of the qualities listed above.

G Fill out the mock evaluation form about your partner. Then switch roles.

Mock Interview Evaluation Form

Name of applicant: _____

Name of interviewer: _____

Date of interview: _____

Job applied for: _____

Rate the applicant on each of the following questions by writing <u>Excellent</u>, <u>Good</u>, or <u>Fair</u>.

What kind of impression did this person make? _____

Did the person give answers that would make an employer want to hire him or her?

_____

Did the person have a friendly, enthusiastic, and positive attitude?

_____

What suggestions can you give this person for how to make a better impression?

_____

Rate the applicant on the criteria below on a scale of 1 to 5.
(1=poor and 5=excellent)

CRITERIA		RATING			
	1	2	3	4	5
1. Handshake	__	__	__	__	__
2. Appearance	__	__	__	__	__
3. Eye contact with interviewer	__	__	__	__	__
4. Voice level (volume)	__	__	__	__	__
5. Facial expressions	__	__	__	__	__
6. Posture / body position	__	__	__	__	__
7. Self-confidence / comfort level	__	__	__	__	__
8. Willingness to volunteer information	__	__	__	__	__
9. Appropriateness of responses to questions	__	__	__	__	__
10. Effectiveness in describing strengths, skills, and abilities	__	__	__	__	__
11. Overall evaluation	__	__	__	__	__

Comments: _____

_____

_____

Review

A **If you want to get a job, what are all the things you need to do from beginning to end? Make a list.**

1. _____   5. _____
2. _____   6. _____
3. _____   7. _____
4. _____   8. _____

B **List three skills that you have. List three skills that you need to work on.**

1. _____   1. _____
2. _____   2. _____
3. _____   3. _____

C **Complete the following sentences by yourself.**

My three best skills are that I'm _____
_____

I need to work on being more _____
_____

D **What should you put on your resume? Make a list.**

_____   _____
_____   _____
_____   _____
_____   _____

E **In this unit, you learned many things about getting a job. With a group discuss each of the following. Come up with one sentence about why each is important. Share your answers with the class.**

Knowing my skills is important because _____

_____

Knowing my interests is important because _____

_____

Finding information about the job I want is important because _____

_____

Finding information about the company I am applying to is important because _____

_____

Writing a resume is important because _____

_____

Writing a cover letter is important because _____

_____

Practicing interviewing is important because _____

_____

 F **Combine the two sentences using an adjective clause.**

1. I need to find a new job. I know it will be hard to find a new job.

   _____

2. Many companies are looking for employees with strong communication skills. Many companies hire customer service personnel.

   _____

 G **Combine the two ideas using past perfect.**

(first) Dinora finished her ESL classes.

(second) Dinora started taking classes for her AA Degree.

_____

(first) Eric applied for a small business loan.

(second) Eric opened his business.

_____

TEAM PROJECT

Create an application portfolio

By yourself, you will create a job application portfolio, which will contain all the information you need to apply for a job and go on a practice interview.

With a team, you will create a job, write a brief job advertisement, and interview students.

1. Make a list of all the information you want to include in your portfolio.

2. Create the different parts of your portfolio. All portfolios must include the following: a resume, a cover letter or application letter, sample interview questions and answers. (Other possible items: certificates, awards, transcripts, performance reviews, letters of recommendation.)

3. Form a team with four or five students. Choose positions for each member of your team.

Position	Job Description	Student Name
Student 1 Leader	See that everyone speaks English. See that everyone participates.	
Student 2 Secretary	Take notes and write job advertisement.	
Student 3 Spokesperson	Ask interview questions.	
Students 4/5 Member (s)	Help secretary and spokesperson with their work.	

4. Decide what company you are and for what position you are hiring. Write a job advertisement for the position. Put all teams' job advertisements on one page to be distributed to the class.

5. Prepare a list of interview questions that you will ask the applicants.

6. Decide what you are looking for in an employee, and create an evaluation form.

7. Interview and evaluate the applicants.

8. Choose the best person for the job.

PRONUNCIATION

Contractions. Would and *had* can both have the contraction *'d* in spoken English and in informal written style. Read the examples below and decide if the contraction *'d* stands for *would* or *had*. Write *would* or *had* in the spaces below. Then listen and repeat each sentence.

1. I'd worked in Australia for three months before I started to feel homesick. _____

2. I'd go to the job center and ask for an application if I were you. _____

3. She'd like to get a job in engineering when she graduates. _____

4. They'd offered him a job before he finished his degree. _____

LEARNER LOG

In this unit, you learned many things about getting hired. How comfortable do you feel doing each of the skills listed below? Rate your comfort level on a scale of 1 to 4.

1 = Not so comfortable **2** = Need more practice **3** = Comfortable **4** = Very comfortable

If you circle 1 or 2, write down the page number where you can review this skill.

Vocabulary	Comfort Level				Page(s)
I can identify job skills and job titles.	1	2	3	4	_____
Life Skill					
I can complete a skills inventory.	1	2	3	4	_____
I can identify job titles and responsibilities.	1	2	3	4	_____
I can conduct a job search.	1	2	3	4	_____
I can conduct a company search.	1	2	3	4	_____
I can write down my job history.	1	2	3	4	_____
I can identify the parts of a resume.	1	2	3	4	_____
I can write a resume.	1	2	3	4	_____
I can write a cover letter.	1	2	3	4	_____
I can prepare for a job interview.	1	2	3	4	_____
I can practice interviewing.	1	2	3	4	_____
Grammar					
I can use adjective clauses.	1	2	3	4	_____
I can use the past perfect.	1	2	3	4	_____

Reflection
Complete the following statements with your thoughts about this unit.

I learned _____

I would like to find out more about _____

I am still confused about _____

On the Job

GOALS

- Discuss appropriate workplace behavior
- Use the passive voice
- Communicate problems to a supervisor
- Use tag questions
- Discuss workplace ethics
- Work out meanings from context
- Write a letter asking for a raise

LESSON 1

Can I wear this to work?

GOAL ▶ Discuss appropriate workplace behavior   *Life skill*

A Imagine that you are at work. Think carefully about each situation below and decide if it is appropriate (A) or inappropriate (I). Write *A* or *I* next to each statement.

_____ Ask a co-worker for help.

_____ Ask for a raise.

_____ Call in sick (when you are really sick).

_____ Send personal e-mails.

_____ Sit on your desk.

_____ Smoke while you're working.

_____ Talk to a friend on the phone.

_____ Do Internet research for your child's school project.

_____ Take products home for your friends and family.

_____ Talk to your supervisor about a problem with a co-worker.

_____ Arrive at work a few minutes late.

_____ Tell your supervisor you don't understand something he or she said.

B Discuss your answers with a group and think of three more examples of appropriate and inappropriate workplace behavior. Share your ideas with the class.

C Read each of the situations below and decide if it is appropriate or inappropriate. Why do you think personal grooming is important in the workplace? Discuss the situations with your partner.

> **groom – v.** to take care of your own appearance by keeping your body, clothes, and hair clean and neat   **n. – grooming**

Alison is an administrative assistant in an office building. She runs every morning before she goes to work. Usually she gets home in time to shower, but this morning she is late. She has to decide between changing her clothes and having breakfast. She decides to skip breakfast today and shower and change into her work clothes.

Alison

Ross

Ross is a mechanic who worked a 14-hour shift yesterday. He was so tired that he went to bed in his work clothes. When he got up in the morning, he didn't have time to shower, but he washed his face, shaved, and put on a clean shirt. He didn't have time to clean his fingernails, but he knew they'd be getting dirty again anyway.

D On a separate sheet of paper, draw a diagram like the one below. Complete the diagram with facts about workplace grooming. Remember that some things are true for both men and women.

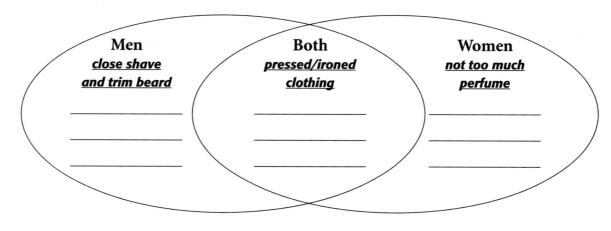

Men	Both	Women
close shave and trim beard	*pressed/ironed clothing*	*not too much perfume*

The note was written by Jim.

GOAL ▶ **Use the passive voice**

> Where are these people?
> What are they talking about?
> What can you see on the desk?

A Listen and read the conversation.

Raquel: Did you see the note I put on your desk?

Bruno: Was that note from you? I thought it was put there by Jim.

Raquel: Actually, the note was written by Jim but I taped it to your desk. I wanted to make sure you got it before you left for lunch.

Bruno: I did get it. The orders were sent to me yesterday and I'll have them ready for your signature before I leave today.

Raquel: Great! I'll sign them in the morning, and then you can send them to the Finance Department. Make sure they are sent by Package Express.

Bruno: I'll take care of it right away.

B Answer the questions about the conversation with a partner.

1. Who are the two people in the conversation? Who is the supervisor?

2. What is the misunderstanding?

3. What was sent to Bruno?

C Practice the conversation, but this time replace some of the words and phrases with the new words below.

desk	→	computer
note	→	memo
lunch	→	the day
Finance Department	→	Human Resources
right away	→	as soon as possible

D **Look at the sentences below. Compare the sentences in the passive voice with those in the active voice. What is the difference?**

Passive voice	Active voice
The note was put there by Raquel.	Raquel put the note there.
The note was written by Jim.	Jim wrote the note.
The orders were sent yesterday. (We don't know who sent them.)	They sent the orders yesterday.

Passive subject	*be*	Past participle	(*by* + person or thing)	Example sentence
I, he, she , it	was	written	by Jim	The note was written by Jim.
you, we, they	were	sent		The orders were sent yesterday. (We don't know who sent them.)

Use the passive voice to emphasize the object of the action or when the doer of the action is unknown or unimportant. To make an active sentence into a passive sentence, switch the subject and the object, and change the verb to the correct tense of *be* + the past participle. The word *by* is used before the doer of the action.

E **Change the following sentences from active voice to passive voice. Think of your own ideas for the final sentence.**

EXAMPLE:
Our delivery person brought twelve bottles of water this morning.
Twelve bottles of water were brought by our delivery person this morning.

1. The receptionist bought all the supplies.

   _____

2. The repairperson fixed the copy machine.

   _____

3. Our supervisor wrote some new regulations.

   _____

4. Someone stole his money and driver's license.

   _____

5. A nurse took my blood pressure.

   _____

6. _____

   _____

LESSON 3 Taking action

| GOAL ▶ | Communicate problems to a supervisor | *Life skill* |

A Listen to the conversation.

Construction worker: Excuse me, do you have a second?

Supervisor: Sure. What is it?

Construction worker: Well, there's a small problem. The shipment of lumber didn't arrive, so we have to stop construction until it gets here. What would you like us to do?

Supervisor: There's nothing else you can do while you are waiting for it?

Construction worker: No. We need that lumber to start working on the door frames.

Supervisor: OK. Well, why don't you guys take lunch early, and I'll call and see where the lumber is?

Construction worker: OK, so you want all of us to go on lunch break right now, while you call and find out where the lumber is?

Supervisor: That's right.

Construction worker: When should we come back?

Supervisor: In about an hour.

Construction worker: Thank you. See you in an hour.

B With a partner, answer the following questions about the conversation.

1. What is the problem?

2. What does the employee say to get the supervisor's attention?

3. Does the supervisor understand the problem?

4. What does she suggest they do to solve the problem?

How to get someone's attention politely	How to check that you have understood
Excuse me, sir/ma'am/ (name). Do you have a minute? Pardon me, sir/ma'am/ (name). Can I talk to you for a second?	Let me make sure I understand you. What you are saying is . . . So what we/I should do is . . .

C **Read the flow chart below. Do you agree with each step?**

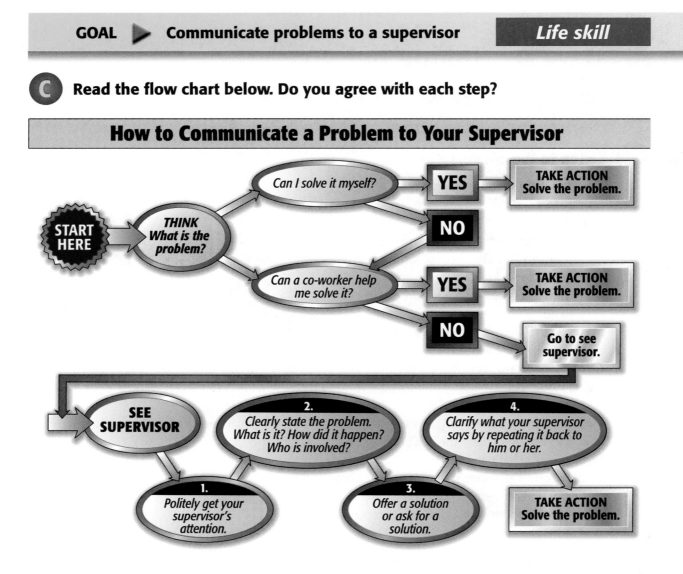

How to Communicate a Problem to Your Supervisor

START HERE

THINK
What is the problem?

Can I solve it myself?
YES → TAKE ACTION Solve the problem.
NO

Can a co-worker help me solve it?
YES → TAKE ACTION Solve the problem.
NO → Go to see supervisor.

SEE SUPERVISOR

1. Politely get your supervisor's attention.

2. Clearly state the problem. What is it? How did it happen? Who is involved?

3. Offer a solution or ask for a solution.

4. Clarify what your supervisor says by repeating it back to him or her.

TAKE ACTION Solve the problem.

D **Discuss these questions with a partner.**

1. If you can solve the problem by yourself, what should you do?

2. If a co-worker can help you solve the problem, what should you do?

3. When you go to see your supervisor, what is the first thing you should do? What is the last thing you should do?

How to suggest a solution
Why don't we/I . . . ?
What if we/ I . . . ?
Would it work if we/ I . . . ?

E **Look at the conversation on the previous page. Did the construction worker follow the steps in the flow chart?**

F **With a group, read each situation below. Following the steps in the flow chart on page 126, discuss what you would do if you were in that situation. Do the first one with your class as an example.**

1. Renee is a cashier in a fast-food restaurant. A customer just came up to the counter and told her that she gave him the wrong change. He doesn't have his receipt and she doesn't remember helping him. What should she do?

2. Mikhail came back from lunch and found a message marked *urgent* that wasn't addressed to him on his desk. He doesn't recognize the name of the addressee so he doesn't know what to do with it. What should he do?

3. James and Sara assemble telephones. For this particular group of phones, they have an uneven number of parts and aren't able to finish 20 of the phones. What should they do?

G **Separate your class into two groups. Read your group's directions.**

Group A: Supervisors
As a group, discuss how you would solve each of the problems in exercise H below. Be prepared to communicate this to your employee when he or she asks you.

Group B: Employees
As a group, discuss what you would say to your supervisor about each of the problems in exercise H below. Remember the four steps from the flow chart.

H **When you are ready, each employee from Group B should find a supervisor from Group A to talk to about the first problem. You must talk to a different supervisor about each problem.**

1. You just received your paycheck and you notice that you didn't get paid for the overtime hours you worked.

2. There is an emergency phone call for you, but if you leave your place, you will throw off the assembly line.

3. You are out installing cable TV at a customer's home and the customer is unhappy with your service.

I **Now, switch! The supervisors will become employees, and the employees will become supervisors.**

You speak English, don't you?

GOAL ▷ **Use tag questions** *Grammar*

A **Compare these two questions. Which question is a tag question?**

"Is Eric looking for new employees for his company?"

I have no idea, but I want to know.

"Eric is looking for new employees for his company, isn't he?"

I'm not 100% sure, but I think this is true.

B **Read the questions and answers about rules for tag questions.**

Tag question: *Eric is looking for new employees for his company, isn't he?*

Q: Why is this called a tag question?
A: Because it's a question tagged onto the end of a sentence.

Q: When do we use tag questions?
A: When we are almost sure something is true, but we want to check and make sure.

Q: When I'm asking a tag question, how do I know if the tag should be positive or negative?
A: If the sentence is positive, the tag is negative. If the sentence is negative, the tag is positive.

Q: What verb tense do I use in the tag?
A: Use the same verb tense in the tag that is used in the beginning of the statement.

C **Study the chart with your teacher.**

Positive statement	Tag	Negative statement	Tag
She works,	doesn't she?	She doesn't work,	does she?
She is working,	isn't she?	She isn't working,	is she?
She worked,	didn't she?	She didn't work,	did she?
She will work,	won't she?	She won't work,	will she?
She is going to work,	isn't she?	She isn't going to work,	is she?
She has worked,	hasn't she?	She hasn't worked,	has she?
She had worked,	hadn't she?	She hadn't worked,	had she?

D **Listen to the tag questions and fill in the circle next to the tag that you hear.**

1. ○ did he   ○ didn't he   ○ don't he   ○ doesn't he
2. ○ won't she   ○ will she   ○ won't we   ○ don't we
3. ○ did they   ○ did he   ○ didn't they   ○ didn't he
4. ○ hasn't she   ○ did she   ○ didn't she   ○ has she
5. ○ are you   ○ aren't you   ○ don't you   ○ were you

E **Complete each of the following questions with the correct tag.**

1. He isn't being promoted, _____

2. Lisa and Jack have never missed a day of work, _____

3. Maria lives near her job, _____

4. Our computers will be repaired next week, _____

5. My assistant is going to get a new office, _____

6. She didn't finish her work, _____

7. The supervisor said to wait until tomorrow to finish, _____

8. The machine broke down, _____

9. Roberto had worked in a restaurant before, _____

10. We'll have a business meeting next week, _____

F **Write four tag questions you might be able to use at your work. If you don't have a job, write tag questions you could use at home or at school.**

EXAMPLE:
She left the package at the office, didn't she?

1. _____

2. _____

3. _____

4. _____

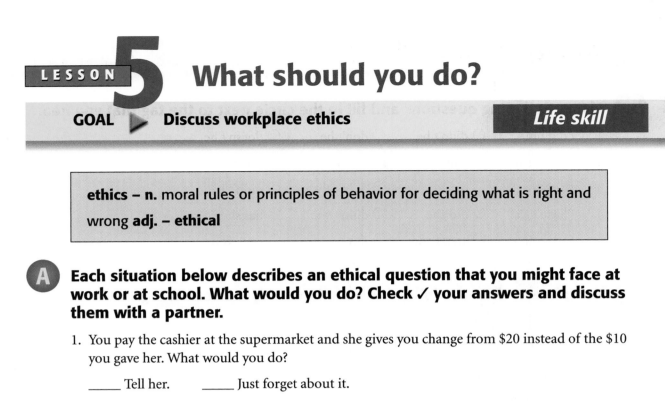

LESSON 5   # What should you do?

| GOAL ▶ Discuss workplace ethics | *Life skill* |

> **ethics – n.** moral rules or principles of behavior for deciding what is right and
> wrong **adj. – ethical**

A   **Each situation below describes an ethical question that you might face at work or at school. What would you do? Check ✓ your answers and discuss them with a partner.**

1. You pay the cashier at the supermarket and she gives you change from $20 instead of the $10 you gave her. What would you do?

   _____ Tell her.   _____ Just forget about it.

2. It's the night before the final exam at your school and you haven't had much time to study. A classmate has stolen the answers to the exam and offers to share them with you. What would you do?

   _____ Say no.   _____ Borrow the answers from him.

3. You go shopping and buy some books. When you get home, you realize that the clerk put an extra book in your bag that you didn't pay for. What would you do?

   _____ Go back to the store and give the book back.   _____ Keep it.

B   **In the examples above, you know what you should do, but do you always do it? Sometimes, the decision is not that easy, but there are steps you can take to help you make a good decision.**

> ### Steps for Making an Ethical Decision
>
> 1. Identify the ethical issue or problem.
> 2. List the facts that are most relevant to your decision.
> 3. Identify the people who might be affected by your decision and how.
> 4. Explain what each person would want you to do about the issue.
> 5. List three different decisions you could make and what the outcome of each decision would be.
> 6. Decide what you will do.

C   **Using the steps above, discuss one of the situations in exercise A with a group and decide what would be the best thing to do.**

D **With a group, choose one of the ethical situations below.**

1.
Ricardo, the night security guard, has access to all of the buildings at night. It is a slow night and he wants to check his personal e-mail using one of the available computers. The company has a strict policy about e-mail being used for business purposes only, but Ricardo is the only person in the building.

3.
Kimberly, who works as a receptionist in the front office, has access to the copy machine to make copies for other employees. Her daughter, Alyse, needs some copies for a school project. She brought her own paper and needs 200 copies for her class. Alyse needs to have the copies or she will fail the project and possibly not pass the class. The company copier does not require a security code and they don't keep track of who made how many copies.

2.
Emilia is a janitor who is in charge of cleaning the restrooms and refilling all of the depleted supplies. She is the only one with a key to the supply closet. Her husband is very sick, and she is having trouble making enough money to support her family. Often times they can't afford food and they can't afford to buy toilet paper and soap.

4.
Brandon works in Quality Control, helping refurbish used computers. Once a year, his supervisor gives away computers to a local elementary school. He doesn't keep any records of this and Brandon really needs a computer for his son who is just starting high school. His supervisor asks him to deliver twelve computers to the local school.

E **For the situation you have chosen, follow the steps for making an ethical decision on page 130. On a separate piece of paper, answer each of the questions below before you make your final decision.**

1. What is the ethical problem?

2. What are the relevant facts?

3. Which people are involved and how would each person be affected?

4. What would each person want you to do?

5. What are three different possible decisions?

6. What is your final decision?

F **Write a description of a situation where you had to make an ethical choice. What did you do? How did you feel afterward?**

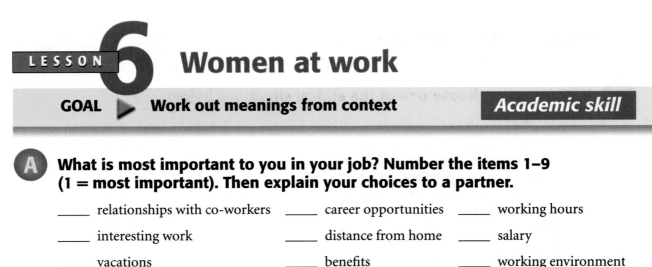

LESSON 6 **Women at work**

A **What is most important to you in your job? Number the items 1–9 (1 = most important). Then explain your choices to a partner.**

_____ relationships with co-workers   _____ career opportunities   _____ working hours

_____ interesting work   _____ distance from home   _____ salary

_____ vacations   _____ benefits   _____ working environment

B **Read the following article about getting a raise. Underline the advice that could be useful for you.**

How to Ask for a Raise

Men are still earning more than women—lots more. According to the most recent Census Bureau data, the pay gap between men and women is 27%—a woman earns 73 cents for every dollar a man earns. What does that mean? A woman works four weeks to earn as much as her male counterpart earns in three weeks.

How can women close the gap? Knock on the boss's door and ask for a raise, because getting the raise is not as difficult as it might seem. Here are 10 tips to assist women in negotiating the annual raise.

1. **Be a star performer.** Make yourself indispensable to the company. Document your successes by saving e-mails and letters, and compiling them into a portfolio. Make sure to take this with you when you go to your boss.
2. **Research.** Know what other men and women in your field are paid.
3. **Focus on your contributions to the company.** While the raise is certainly important to you, do not focus on how it will help your credit card debt.
4. **Be informed.** Know the company's policy on raises by asking your human resources director.
5. **Timing is everything.** Don't ask when the office is hectic. Wait until the pace

has slowed down and the moment is right.
6. **Do your homework.** Rehearse and prepare responses to counter any objections your boss might have. Know ahead of time what the difficult questions might be and have your answers ready!
7. **Rehearse.** If you can, act out the scenario with a friend or colleague. This will help you to become more comfortable when you are actually doing the asking.
8. **Be a professional.** Ask for a formal meeting with your boss.
9. **Cover your bases.** Make four points about your contribution prior to asking for the raise. Illustrate your ability:
   - to find solutions,
   - to go above and beyond your job responsibilities,
   - to help others, and most importantly,
   - to increase the company's profitability.
10. **Don't take no for an answer.** Negotiate more vacation time, stock options, 401K contributions, or flex time. Set goals and ask for another review in three months.

C **Practice working out meaning from context. Use the following steps.**

1. Skim through the article again and circle any words or phrases that you don't understand.

2. Now look at the context and see if you can figure out the meaning on your own. Ask students next to you for help if you need it.

3. Is it necessary to understand these phrases or can you still get the general idea?

4. Ask your teacher or use a dictionary for help with any phrases that you can't figure out.

D **Look at these words from the article. Each word has two meanings. Find the word and choose the correct meaning in this context.**

EXAMPLE:
document
○ paper   ● prove

1. **illustrate**
   ○ give evidence   ○ draw pictures

2. **counter**
   ○ respond to   ○ work surface

3. **contributions**
   ○ money   ○ work or effort

4. **field**
   ○ specialization   ○ grassy area

E **What are the opposites of the words below?**

EXAMPLE:
necessary → **_unnecessary_**

1. dispensable → _____   3. comfortable → _____

2. important → _____   4. formal → _____

F **Discuss the following questions with a group.**

1. This article focuses on how women should ask for a raise. Do you think these same ideas apply to men? Why or why not?

2. Which aspect of asking for a raise do you think is the most difficult? Take a poll in your group.

G **Nabil met with his boss yesterday to ask for a raise. Read about his experience.**

Nabil has been working for EJ Electronics as an assembler for two years. In the past year, he has come up with new ways to make the assembly line more efficient and helped increase productivity in his department. Nabil thinks he deserves a raise. He has friends that work at other electronics companies and he has been finding out what different employees are paid. He believes that with his experience and his contributions to the company, his boss should give him a raise.

First, Nabil went to see Heidi in Human Resources and asked her what procedures he needed to follow to ask for a raise. She suggested that he make an appointment with his boss. So last week, he asked his boss if the two of them could sit down and have a meeting. When his boss agreed, he began to gather his paperwork: job evaluations, memos from his supervisor about the new assembly line configurations, his "Employee of the Month" award, and records of his attendance at work. He sat down and thought about all the questions his boss might ask him and he wrote out detailed answers. Then he asked his cousin to practice asking him those questions.

H **Look back at the article on page 132. How did Nabil follow each point from the article? Some things are not mentioned in the story about Nabil. How do you think he handled those aspects of asking for a raise?**

I **Imagine you are Nabil. Practice the conversation he might rehearse with his cousin. Then act out the conversation with his boss.**

J **Active Task:** Find a friend or family member and rehearse asking for a raise.

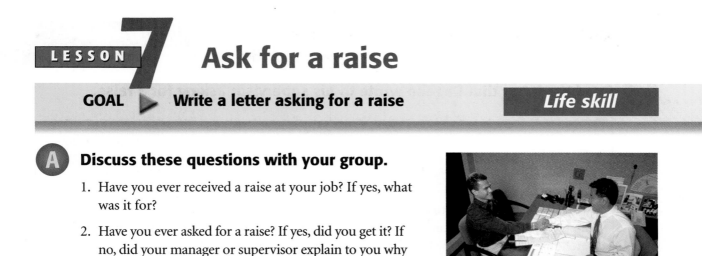

LESSON 7 — Ask for a raise

GOAL ▶ **Write a letter asking for a raise**

A **Discuss these questions with your group.**

1. Have you ever received a raise at your job? If yes, what was it for?

2. Have you ever asked for a raise? If yes, did you get it? If no, did your manager or supervisor explain to you why you didn't get it?

B **Many people hesitate to ask for a raise. Can you think of some reasons why? Make list below.**

_____

_____

_____

C **Let's get ready to ask for a raise! First of all, answer the following questions on a separate piece of paper. (If you are a homemaker or a student, imagine that you get paid for what you do and are asking for more money.)**

1. Do you deserve a raise? Why or why not?

2. How long have you been working at your job?

3. When was the last time you got a raise?

4. Have you been working harder or working more hours?

5. Have you been given more responsibilities?

6. Have you gotten good reviews from your supervisors?

D **You can ask for a raise in person or by writing a letter. What do you think the advantages and disadvantages of each are?**

Ask for a raise in person		Ask for a raise by writing	
Advantages	Disadvantages	Advantages	Disadvantages

E **Read the letter that Rogelio wrote to his supervisor asking for a raise.**

August 14, 2002

Dear Mr. Michalski,

   I'm writing this letter to ask you to consider giving me a raise. I have been working at Mitchell George Manufacturing for five years and I really like my job here. I started out as a warehouse packer, and now I work in the shipping department.
   I feel like I deserve a raise because in the past year I have been given more responsibilities on my shift. I have trained ten new employees and become a team leader. I have increased efficiency in my department by implementing a new flow system that helps us pack and ship the boxes in less time. Therefore, I hope that you will consider giving me a raise.
   I would like to sit down and discuss this with you as soon as it is convenient for you. Thank you for your time.

Sincerely,
Rogelio Rodriguez

F **Read the letter again and check which of the following Rogelio included in his letter.**

_____ date

_____ a thank you to his supervisor for reading the letter

_____ greeting

_____ reason for writing the letter

_____ how long he has been working for the company

_____ what his job is

_____ how his job has changed since he has been there

_____ things he has done to help the company

_____ closing

G **Write a letter asking for a raise. Include each part mentioned above.**

Review

A Add tags to the following statements to make tag questions.

1. In this unit, we were taught how to read a flow chart, _____

2. They understand how to make ethical decisions, _____

3. You have learned how to ask for a raise, _____

4. They didn't study computer science in school, _____

5. In the next unit, our teacher will teach us about civics, _____

6. Tag questions are easy, _____

B Take each group of words and write a sentence in the passive voice. You may have to add some words.

EXAMPLE:
new office building / build / Lynn Street
A new office building was built on Lynn Street.

1. childcare workers / give / a raise

    _____

2. machines / repair / mechanics

    _____

3. roses / cut / gardeners

    _____

4. this computer / buy / the finance department

    _____

5. reports / write / two weeks ago

    _____

6. package / sent / express mail

    _____

C Match the questions and the answers below.

_____ 1. Why don't we phone human resources?   a. Let me know right away.

_____ 2. Could I speak to you for a second?   b. That's right.

_____ 3. So what we should do is find another office? c. Yes, what do you need?

_____ 4. What should we do if we run out of supplies? d. That's a good idea.

Review

 D Recall what you learned about each of the following topics. Without looking back in the book, what is the most important thing you learned about each?

Topic	The most important thing I learned
Workplace behavior and grooming	
Communicating problems to supervisors	
Workplace ethics	
Asking for a raise	

E Explain what you wrote in the chart to a partner. If your partner wrote something different, add his or her idea to your chart.

F Make a list of four new words or phrases from this unit that you'd like to use. Write a definition and sentence for each.

1. Word: _____

   Definition: _____

   Sentence: _____

2. Word: _____

   Definition: _____

   Sentence: _____

3. Word: _____

   Definition: _____

   Sentence: _____

4. Word: _____

   Definition: _____

   Sentence: _____

T E A M
P R O J E C T

Solve a company problem

With a team, you will solve a company problem in an action committee and create a handout for the class.

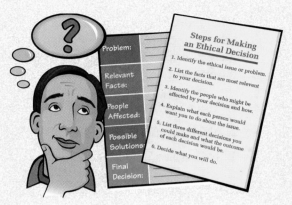

Steps for Making an Ethical Decision
1. Identify the ethical issue or problem.
2. List the facts that are most relevant to your decision.
3. Identify the people who might be affected by your decision and how.
4. Explain what each person would want you to do about the issue.
5. List three different decisions you could make and what the outcome of each decision would be.
6. Decide what you will do.

1. Form a human resources action committee with four or five students. Choose positions for each member of your team.

Position	Job Description	Student Name
Student 1 Leader	See that everyone speaks English. See that everyone participates.	
Student 2 Secretary	Take notes and write information for handout.	
Student 3 Spokesperson	Report your decision to the class.	
Students 4/5 Member (s)	Help secretary and spokesperson with their work.	

2. With your group, carefully read the problem below.

3. Use the steps for making an ethical decision on page 130 to go through each possible solution.

4. Make a final decision.

5. Create a handout explaining the process you went through to come up with your decision.

6. Report your final decision to the class.

Company: RB Aerospace—Refurbishes and designs airplane interiors

Problem: A group of employees discovers that the quality of some of the parts they are using is not up to standard. They are worried that this may cause safety problems when the aircraft is in use. They have mentioned it to the quality control supervisor, but the factory is on a tight schedule and if they don't deliver this contract on time, they may lose future contracts.

PRONUNCIATION

Intonation. In tag questions, a rising intonation often indicates that you are unsure of the answer, and a falling intonation indicates that you are almost sure of the answer. Listen to these examples and decide if they are rising or falling. Draw arrows on the sentences as in the examples.

1. You work in the library, don't you?
2. She is an engineer, isn't she?
3. He hasn't applied yet, has he?
4. We called them, didn't we?
5. You weren't in the office, were you?
6. He wasn't fired, was he?

LEARNER LOG

In this unit, you learned many things about being on the job. How comfortable do you feel doing each of the skills listed below? Rate your comfort level on a scale of 1 to 4.

1 = Not so comfortable **2** = Need more practice **3** = Comfortable **4** = Very comfortable

If you circle 1 or 2, write down the page number where you can review this skill.

Vocabulary	Comfort Level	Page(s)
I can use vocabulary to ask for a raise.	1 2 3 4	_____

Life Skill		
I can discuss workplace behavior and grooming.	1 2 3 4	_____
I can communicate problems to a supervisor.	1 2 3 4	_____
I can discuss workplace ethics.	1 2 3 4	_____
I can make ethical decisions.	1 2 3 4	_____
I can write a letter asking for a raise.	1 2 3 4	_____

Grammar		
I can use the passive voice in the simple past.	1 2 3 4	_____
I can use tag questions.	1 2 3 4	_____

Academic		
I can interpret a flow chart.	1 2 3 4	_____
I can work out meanings from context.	1 2 3 4	_____
I can analyze what I've read.	1 2 3 4	_____

Reflection

Complete the following statements with your thoughts from this unit.

I learned _____

I would like to find out more about _____

I am still confused about _____

UNIT 8 Civic Responsibility

GOALS

- Understand civic responsibility
- Apply for a driver's license
- Respond to a jury summons
- Fill out a tax form
- Interpret a flow chart
- Write a letter about a community problem
- Use passive modals

LESSON 1 — Responsibilities

GOAL ▶ Understand civic responsibility

Life skill

A Why are these things important? Complete the sentences below.

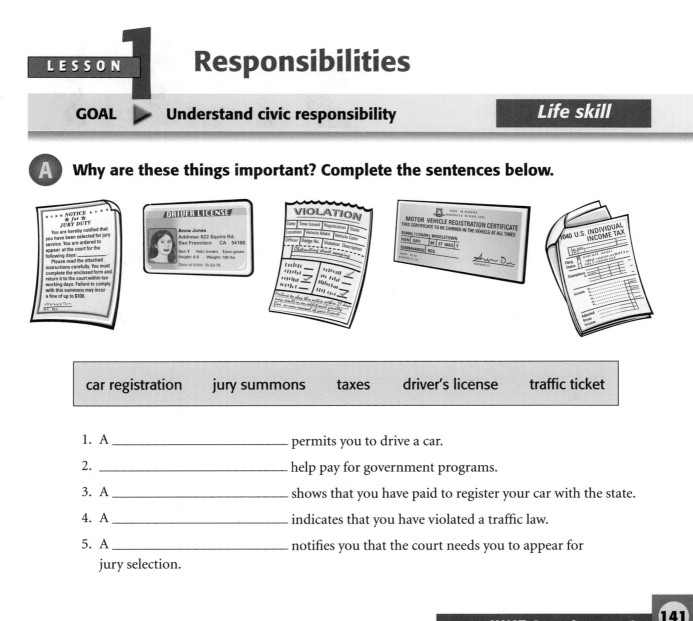

| car registration | jury summons | taxes | driver's license | traffic ticket |

1. A _____ permits you to drive a car.

2. _____ help pay for government programs.

3. A _____ shows that you have paid to register your car with the state.

4. A _____ indicates that you have violated a traffic law.

5. A _____ notifies you that the court needs you to appear for jury selection.

B **A group of students from all over the country are attending a workshop about civic responsibility in the United States. Read their conversation and see if you can define *civic responsibility* with your teacher.**

Bita: I never realized how difficult it would be to get adjusted to life in the United States. There are so many things to do.

Consuela: I know. Getting a driver's license and registering my car was very complicated.

Ranjit: In New York we have good public transportation, so I don't have to worry about a car. But I did get a jury summons the other day and I didn't know what I was supposed to do with it.

Ricardo: I got one of those last year and I couldn't understand it, so I threw it away.

Bita: You threw it away? You can't do that. You have to respond.

Consuela : What about tickets? The other day, I got a ticket for jaywalking. I want to fight it, but I don't know where to go.

Ranjit: I think you have to go to court, don't you?

Bita: The most confusing thing I've had to do is pay taxes. Can't they make those forms easier to understand?

Consuela: I agree. Last year, we paid someone to do our taxes.

C **What five situations do the students mention? Can you think of other situations you've had to deal with in the United States?**

D **With a partner, practice asking about the civic responsibilities listed.**

EXAMPLE:
Student A: Why is a driver's license important?
Student B: It permits you to drive a car.

E **Have you had to deal with the civic responsibilities listed above? What other responsibilities have you had to deal with? Make a list.**

_____   _____

_____   _____

_____   _____

F **Active Task:** Talk to a friend or family member about civic responsibility.

A driver's license

| GOAL ▶ | **Apply for a driver's license** | *Life skill* |

A Do you have a driver's license? How did you get it? Share your experience with a group of students.

B Bita telephones Consuela to ask about how to get a driver's license. Listen to the conversation and write answers (in your own words) to each of Bita's questions.

1. If I already have my driver's license from another country, do I still have to take the test?

   _____

2. How do I prepare for the written test? _____

   _____

3. How many questions are on the test? _____

4. How many questions do I have to get correct? _____

   _____

5. What if I don't pass it the first time? _____

   _____

6. What do I need to know about the driving test? _____

   _____

   _____

7. How do I apply for the license? _____

   _____

8. Do I need to make an appointment to turn in my application? _____

   _____

9. What do I have to do when I turn in my application? _____

   _____

   _____

10. How much does it cost? _____

C With a partner, practice asking and answering the questions above.

D   **Bita went to the Department of Motor Vehicles (DMV) and got a driver's license application. Fill out the application with help from your teacher.**

DRIVER'S LICENSE APPLICATION

Name:	

Street/PO Box

City	State	Zip

Date of Birth	Sex: ❑ Male ❑ Female	Height	Weight

License Number	Social Security No.	Restricted Code
	Eye Color ❑ Blue ❑ Brown ❑ Black ❑ Green ❑ Gray ❑ Violet ❑ Hazel	

Do you have any condition which might affect your ability to operate a motor vehicle, such as:

❑ Seizures or Unconsciousness	❑ Hearing or Vision Problem	❑ Have Your Driving Privileges Ever Been Suspended?
❑ Mental Disability	❑ Alcohol or Drug Problem	

***If any of the above are checked, a letter of explanation must accompany this application. Failure to do so may delay your license.

I certify that the above statements are true. Do you wish to be an organ donor? ❑ Yes ❑ No

Signed X	Date

Please check one of the following:
❑ Regular Driver's License (Class E)
❑ Out-of-State Transfer
   (Must surrender license from other state.)
❑ Applicant Under Age of 18
   *Must Provide School Enrollment Form
   *License Will Expire on 21st Birthday

DUPLICATE LICENSE FEE: $5.00
❑ Duplicate License
❑ Duplicate Class D License
❑ Address change: If you move, you must change your address on your driver's license within twenty days.
❑ Name Change: [_____]
                     FORMER NAME
*You must attach a copy of your marriage certificate, divorce decree, court order or birth certificate when changing your name.

DEPARTMENT USE ONLY
Your birth certificate must be shown to the examining officer as proof of your age.
The Applicant Named in This Application Passed the Examination Conducted.
At _____ Detachment This _____ Day of _____ 20 ___

Examiner   Unit Number
Restrictions _____

E   **With a group, write a paragraph or make a chart that explains step-by-step how to get a driver's license. Compare your paragraph or chart with another group's.**

F   **Active Task:** Go to the DMV and pick up a driver's handbook and a driver's license application.

GOAL ▶ **Respond to a jury summons**

A **Bita and Ranjit are chatting about jury duty in the United States. Read their conversation.**

Ranjit: Bita, you said we shouldn't throw away a jury summons like Ricardo did. Can you tell me what I'm supposed to do with it?

Bita: Sure. I've had at least three of them.

Ranjit: What are they about, anyway?

Bita: Well, in the United States, anyone accused of a crime has the right to a fair trial, which means a judge and twelve people on a jury listen to the case and make a decision.

Ranjit: Oh, I get it. So can anyone be on a jury?

Bita: No, you have to meet certain qualifications.

Ranjit: Like what?

Bita: First of all, you have to be a U.S. citizen and a resident of the county where the trial is taking place. Also, you have to be able to understand and speak enough English to participate in the jury selection and the trial.

Ranjit: Well, I think I can speak and understand enough English, but I'm not a citizen yet. Does that disqualify me?

Bita: I'm afraid so.

Ranjit: Too bad. It sounds interesting to participate in a trial. So what do I do with this form?

Bita: There should be a series of yes or no questions on it. Answer each of the questions truthfully. Then explain at the bottom why you are not qualified to participate. Some people who are citizens can be excused for other reasons, like financial hardship, medical conditions, or being older than 65. So just fill out the form and then send it back in within 10 days.

Ranjit: That's it?

Bita: That's it. Easy, huh?

B **Discuss the following terms with your teacher. See if you can work out their meanings from the conversation above and by looking at the picture.**

trial	judge
accused of a crime	jury
jury selection	qualifications
attorney	witness
juror	

C Go over the jury summons with your teacher.

JURY SUMMONS

Please bring this upper portion with you when you report for jury duty.

JUROR	You are hereby notified that you have been selected for jury service in the State Trial Courts of _____ County. You are ordered to appear at the court for the following days: *May 3, 4, 5* Your Group Number: 75 Your Juror Number: 567

- -

JUROR QUALIFICATION FORM
DETACH THIS HALF AND RETURN BY MAIL WITHIN 10 DAYS

Name _____

Address _____

City/State/Zip _____

Home Phone _____ Date of Birth _____

Employer _____

Occupation _____

Work Phone _____

Answer each of the following questions under penalty of perjury.

1. Are you a citizen of the United States? ☐ yes ☐ no
2. Are you currently a resident of _____ County? ☐ yes ☐ no
3. Are you 18 years of age or older? ☐ yes ☐ no
4. Do you read, write, speak, and understand the English language? (If another person filled out this form, please provide their name, address, and the reasons in the space provided below.) ☐ yes ☐ no
5. Have you ever been convicted or plead guilty to theft or any felony offense? ☐ yes ☐ no
6. Do you have a physical or mental disability that would interfere with or prevent you from serving as a juror? ☐ yes ☐ no
7. Are you 65 years of age or older? ☐ yes ☐ no

If you answered NO to questions 1, 2, 3, or 4, you are automatically excused from jury duty. Please write your reason below and send in the form.

Reason I cannot serve on jury duty: _____

_____

_____

D Fill out this jury summons with your personal information. What should you do with this form when you have filled it out?

GOAL ▶ **Fill out a tax form**   *Life skill*

A This year Ricardo and Consuela have decided to fill out their own tax forms. Look at the words below and discuss them with your teacher. Look at page 163 to check their meanings.

income	W2 form	owe	refund	overpaid	tax return
exemption	spouse	dependent	withhold	joint or separate	

B Read each portion of the form on the following two pages and do the exercises that follow.

Form **1040** **U.S. Individual Income Tax Return** 20**03**

Label

L A B E L | Your first name and initial Consuela E. | Last name Sanchez | Your social security number XXX : XX : XXXX |
| If a joint return, spouse's first name and initial Ricardo H. | Last name Sanchez | Spouse's social security number XXX : XX : XXXX |

H E R E | Home address (number and street). 2000 Second Avenue | Apt. no. # 1 | ▲ **Important!** ▲ You must enter your SSN(s) above. |
| City, town or post office, state, and ZIP code Loronado, CA 92117 | | |

Filing Status

Check only one box.

1	☐	Single
2	☐	Married filing joint return (even if only one had income)
3	☐	Married filing separate return. Enter spouse's ss# above and full name here. ▶ _____
4	☐	Head of household
5	☐	Qualifying widow(er) with dependent child (year spouse died _____)

C Consuela and Ricardo both work and are filing the same tax return. Put a check in the correct box for them. Which box would you check if this were your tax return? Discuss the choices with your teacher.

Exemptions

6a	☐	**Yourself.** If your parent (or someone else) can claim you as a dependent on his or her tax return, **do not** check box 6a		
b	☐	**Spouse**		
c	☐	**Dependents**		**(3)** Relationship to you
		(1) First name Last name	**(2)** SS#	
			:	
			:	
			:	
			:	
d		Total number of exemptions claimed		

D Consuela is filing the tax return for herself, Ricardo, and their three children, Erica, Frankie, and Justin. Fill out the *Exemptions* portion above with information from the Sanchez family. How many exemptions will they get?

E **Look at the information below and answer the following questions.**

Income	7	Wages, salaries, tips, etc. Attach Form(s) W–2	7	40,968	79
	8	Taxable interest	8	36	79
	9	Add the amounts for lines 7 and 8. This is your total income.	9		

1. How much did the Sanchez family earn at their jobs last year? _____

2. How much interest did they get from their savings? _____

3. What is their total income?_____ Write this number in the form.

 F **Help Consuela fill out the *Tax and Credits* portion below by following the instructions on each line. You will need to consult the tax table below to fill in line 15.**

Tax and Credits Standard Deduction Single: $4,400 Head of Household: $6,450 Married Filing Jointly or Qualifying Widow(er): $7,350 Married Filing Separately: $3,675	10	Amount from line 9	10		
	11	Enter your standard deduction from the left.	11		
	12	Subtract line 11 from line 10	12		
	13	If line 10 is less than $96,700, multiply $2,800 by the total number of exemptions claimed on line 6d	13		
	14	Subtract line 13 from line 12. This is your taxable income. If line 13 is more than line 12, enter 0.	14		
	15	Tax (see tax table)	15		
Payments	16	Federal income tax withheld from forms W–2	16	3320	38
Refund	17	If line 16 is more than line 15, subtract line 15 from line 16. This is the amount you overpaid. You will receive a refund.	17		
Amount You Owe	18	If line 15 is more than line 16, subtract line 16 from line 15. This is the amount you owe.	18		

G **Will the Sanchez family owe taxes or get a refund?**

_____

2003 Tax Table

At least	But less than	Single	Married filing jointly	Married filing separately	Head of a houshold
			Your tax is—		
19,000					
19,400	19,450	2,914	2,914	2,914	2,914
19,450	19,500	2,921	2,921	2,921	2,921
19,500	19,550	2,929	2,929	2,929	2,929
19,550	19,600	2,936	2,936	2,936	2,936
19,600	19,650	2,944	2,944	2,944	2,944
19,650	19,700	2,951	2,951	2,951	2,951
19,700	19,750	2,959	2,959	2,959	2,959
19,750	19,800	2,966	2,966	2,966	2,966

H Imagine that you are single and have no dependents. Fill out the tax form below. Sample numbers have been filled in for you.

Form **1040** U.S. Individual Income Tax Return 20**03**

Label

LABEL HERE	Your first name and initial	Last name		Your social security number
	If a joint return, spouse's first name and initial	Last name		Spouse's social security number
	Home address (number and street).		Apt. no.	▲ **Important!** ▲
	City, town or post office, state, and ZIP code			You must enter your SSN(s) above.

Filing Status

Check only one box.

1 ☐ Single
2 ☐ Married filing joint return (even if only one had income)
3 ☐ Married filing separate return. Enter spouse's ss# above and full name here. ▶ _____
4 ☐ Head of household
5 ☐ Qualifying widow(er) with dependent child (year spouse died _____)

Exemptions

6a ☐ **Yourself.** If your parent (or someone else) can claim you as a dependent on his or her tax return, **do not** check box 6a

b ☐ **Spouse**

c ☐ **Dependents**

(1) First name Last name	(2) SS#	(3) Relationship to you

d Total number of exemptions claimed

Income

7	Wages, salaries, tips, etc. Attach Form(s) W–2	7	29,654	32
8	Taxable interest	8	12	70
9	Add the amounts for lines 7 and 8. This is your total income.	9		

Tax and Credits

Standard Deduction
Single: $4,400
Head of Household: $6,450
Married Filing Jointly or Qualifying Widow(er): $7,350
Married Filing Separately: $3,675

10	Amount from line 9	10	
11	Enter your standard deduction from the left.	11	
12	Subtract line 11 from line 10	12	
13	If line 10 is less than $96,700, multiply $2,800 by the total number of exemptions claimed on line 6d	13	
14	Subtract line 13 from line 12. This is your taxable income. If line 13 is more than line 12, enter 0.	14	
15	Tax (see tax schedule)	15	

Payments

16	Federal income tax withheld from forms W–2	16	3,320	38

Refund

17	If line 16 is more than line 15, subtract line 15 from line 16. This is the amount you overpaid. You will receive a refund.	17	

Amount You Owe

18	If line 15 is more than line 16, subtract line 16 from line 15. This is the amount you owe.	18	

2003 Tax Table

At least	But less than	Single	Married filing jointly	Married filing separately	Head of a houshold
				Your tax is—	
24,000					
24,400	24,450	3,664	3,664	3,892	3,664
24,450	24,500	3,671	3,671	3,906	3,671
24,500	24,550	3,679	3,679	3,919	3,679
24,550	24,600	3,686	3,686	3,933	3,686
24,600	24,650	3,694	3,694	3,947	3,694
24,650	24,700	3,701	3,701	3,961	3,701
24,700	24,750	3,709	3,709	3,974	3,709
24,750	24,800	3,716	3,716	3,988	3,716

Elections

GOAL ▶ Interpret a flow chart *Academic skill*

A The students are chatting about local elections. Read their conversation. Do you agree with the speakers? Why is it important to understand the electoral process?

Ranjit: Elections for a new mayor are coming up here in New York. Have any of you participated in an election before?

Bita: I have. I just became a U.S. citizen last year, so I finally got to vote.

Ricardo: So if we're not citizens, we don't need to pay attention to the elections, do we?

Bita: Oh, I disagree. Even when I wasn't a citizen, I participated in local town meetings and city council meetings.

Consuela: Why?

Bita: Because I live in this community just like everyone else, and I want my voice to be heard.

Ranjit: I agree with you, Bita. I think it's important that we voice our opinions on local issues in our community. I've been listening to the candidates' speeches to see who I would vote for. But I don't really understand how the election process works.

Bita: Let's look at the chart our teacher gave us.

B Read the flow chart and discuss it with your class.

1 An elected position becomes available. POSSIBLE REASONS:
1. TERM IS UP
2. SOMEONE STEPS DOWN
3. SOMEONE DIES

2 NOMINATIONS People decide to run and are nominated by their party for the position.

3 CAMPAIGN These people campaign by speaking in public and raising money.

4 ELECTIONS Registered voters vote for the candidate they have chosen.

5 The ballots are counted.

6 The winner is announced.

C Explain the words in the box to your partner. Then have your partner explain the electoral process to you using these words.

elected	position	to step down	term	ballots	to announce

D Write a paragraph about the electoral process. Use some of these sequencing transitions in your paragraph.

Next,	Finally,	First of all,
After that,	In conclusion,	Secondly,
At the next stage,	In summary,	Thirdly,

_____

_____

_____

_____

_____

_____

_____

_____

_____

_____

_____

_____

_____

_____

_____

_____

_____

_____

_____

LESSON 6   Problems in your community

GOAL ▶ Write a letter about a community problem   *Life skill*

A Look at the photos below and identify what these local community problems might be. Discuss some possible solutions for each problem with your group.

1.

3.

2.

4.

B List each problem below. Write one solution for each problem.

Problems	Solutions
1.	
2.	
3.	
4.	

C Share your solutions with the class and, as a class, come up with the best solution for each problem.

D **Prepare to write a business letter about a problem in your community. Choose one of the problems you discussed with your group or a problem in your own community. Before writing the letter, fill in the information below.**

Date: _____

Your name and address: _____
_____

Official's name and address (Research this information.): _____
_____

State the problem: _____
_____
_____
_____

Facts or anecdotes about the problem: _____
_____
_____
_____

Suggested solutions: _____
_____
_____

Closing: _____

E **Choose one of the problems and solutions that you discussed on the previous page and write a letter to a local official. Format it like a business letter.**

LESSON 7 What's your platform?

| GOAL ▷ Use passive modals | *Grammar* |

A Listen to the speeches from three people running for mayor of your city. For the first speech, put a check next to everything the candidate promises to do for you. For the second two speeches, write down what they promise to do for you. You will hear each speech two times.

Antonio Juliana promises to:

❑ clean up the streets

❑ lower tuition fees

❑ improve public transportation

❑ decrease gang violence

❑ get kids off the streets

❑ help the homeless people

❑ increase environmental awareness

Antonio Juliana

Gary Hurt promises to:

1. clean up the beaches

2. _____

   _____

3. _____

Gary Hurt

Kwan Tan promises to:

1. _____

2. _____

3. _____

4. _____

Kwan Tan

B Who would you vote for if you were interested in:

the environment? _____

education? _____

safe streets? _____

C **Read Kwan Tan's speech.**

Good evening, and thank you for coming tonight! This community has given me so many opportunities and, in running for mayor, I hope to give something back to the city that welcomed me as an immigrant, educated me through my teen years, and supported me as I opened my first business.

First on my agenda is education. I will make sure your tax dollars are used to build more schools, so our children won't have to sit in overcrowded classrooms. I'll lower the tuition at our community colleges, so all of us will have a chance to continue our education. I'll implement standards to ensure that schools are teaching our kids what they need to know. I'll start a parent-involvement program that encourages parents to participate actively in their kids' schools. Our children are the future of our community, and we should invest time and money in their success.

Vote for me on Election Day and you'll have schools and a community to be proud of!

Kwan Tan for Mayor

Kwan Tan is:
- ☑ A local business owner
- ☑ A member of this community for over 25 years
- ☑ A parent of two school-age children

A vote for Kwan will ensure for our community:
- ➡ More primary and secondary schools
- ➡ Improved standards of education
- ➡ More parent involvement in schools
- ➡ Lower community college tuition

☑ **Vote for Kwan Tan**

D **Write sentences to describe the issues Kwan Tan wants to change. Use noun clauses following the example below.**

EXAMPLE:
Kwan Tan wants to build more schools.
She thinks that ___more schools should be built.___

1. Kwan Tan wants to lower tuition fees at community colleges.

She says that _____

2. Kwan Tan wants to implement standards in schools.

She thinks that _____

3. Kwan Tan wants to encourage parents to participate in their kids' schools.

She believes that _____

4. Kwan Tan wants to invest time and money in children.

She emphasizes that _____

Study the chart below with your teacher.

Passive modals				
Passive subject	**Modal**	***be***	**Past participle**	**Example sentence**
Schools	should	be	built	More schools should be built.
Taxes	need to	be	increased	Taxes need to be increased.
Children	must	be	protected	Children must be protected.
Parents	have to	be	involved	Parents have to be involved.

 Think of three problems you would like to solve in your community. Write three sentences using passive modals.

1. _____

2. _____

3. _____

 Kwan's election speech has three parts. Look for each part in her speech on page 155.

Introduction   She introduces herself and explains why she is running for office.

Body   She tells her audience what she plans to do if she is elected.

Conclusion   She reminds her audience to vote and tells them once again what changes she will make to the community.

 Imagine you are running for mayor of your community. How would you introduce yourself? What problems would you like to solve? On a separate sheet of paper, write a speech that you would give if you were running for mayor. Practice it and give your speech to the class.

Active Task: Look in the newspaper or on the Internet to find who is mayor or who is running for mayor in your town or city. What issues are they concerned about? What problems do they want to solve?

Review

A Recall what you learned about each of the following topics. Without looking back in the book, what is the most important thing you learned about each?

Topic	The most important thing I learned
A jury summons	
A driver's license	
Income tax	
Community problems	
The electoral process	

B Are the following statements true or false?

○ True ○ False   You have to be 18 to apply for a driver's license.

○ True ○ False   You must reply to a jury summons.

○ True ○ False   You have to be a U.S. citizen to serve on a jury.

○ True ○ False   Everyone must file his or her income tax return separately.

○ True ○ False   If you pay too much tax, the government will give you a refund.

○ True ○ False   Only U.S. citizens can get involved in the community.

C What are three problems in your community you'd like to solve? How would you solve them?

Problem	Solution
1.	
2.	
3.	

 Rewrite each of these sentences using a passive modal.

1. We must protect the environment.

_____

2. They should reduce our taxes.

_____

3. They need to invest money in our educational system.

_____

4. We have to reduce the driving speed limit.

_____

 Make a list of three new words or phrases from this unit that you'd like to use. Write a definition and sentence for each.

1. Word: _____

   Definition: _____

   Sentence: _____

2. Word: _____

   Definition: _____

   Sentence: _____

3. Word: _____

   Definition: _____

   Sentence: _____

F **How have your learning strategies improved during this course? Make a list of ways you have improved your strategies for learning.**

Vocabulary: _____

_____

Grammar: _____

_____

Life Skills: _____

_____

Academic Skills: _____

_____

Conduct an election

With a team, you will prepare a candidate for an election. As a class, you will conduct an election.

1. Form a campaign committee with four or five students. Choose positions for each member of your team.

Position	Job Description	Student Name
Student 1 Leader	See that everyone speaks English. See that everyone participates.	
Student 2 Secretary	Take notes and write candidate's speech.	
Student 3 Presidential candidate	Give speech to class.	
Students 4/5 Member (s)	Help secretary and candidate with their work.	

2. With your team, decide who will be running for class president. Announce the nomination to the class.

3. Members: Create a ballot with all the nominees' names on it. Make a ballot box for students to put their ballots in after they vote.

4. Decide what issues are most important and write a campaign speech.

5. Candidates give speeches to the class.

6. Vote.

7. Count the ballots and announce the winner.

PRONUNCIATION

Intonation. We use a falling-rising intonation when information is less important, and a falling intonation when it is more important. Listen to each sentence below and mark the intonation of each clause with an arrow. Add your own example for number 4.

1. I don't believe in the death penalty, but I think violent criminals should be punished.

2. If more training were available, there wouldn't be so many unemployed people.

3. If people don't vote, they shouldn't complain about who gets elected.

4. _____

LEARNER LOG

In this unit, you learned many things about civic responsibility. How comfortable do you feel doing each of the skills listed below? Rate your comfort level on a scale of 1 to 4.
1 = Not so comfortable **2** = Need more practice **3** = Comfortable **4** = Very comfortable
If you circle 1 or 2, write down the page number where you can review this skill.

Life Skill	Comfort Level				Page(s)
I can apply for a driver's license.	1	2	3	4	_____
I can respond to a jury summons.	1	2	3	4	_____
I can fill out a tax form.	1	2	3	4	_____
I can identify community problems and possible solutions.	1	2	3	4	_____
I can write a letter to a local official about a community problem.	1	2	3	4	_____
I can communicate opinions about community issues.	1	2	3	4	_____

Grammar

I can use noun clauses.	1	2	3	4	_____
I can use passives with modals.	1	2	3	4	_____

Academic

I can interpret a flow chart about the electoral process.	1	2	3	4	_____
I can explain the electoral process.	1	2	3	4	_____
I can understand key points of a speech.	1	2	3	4	_____
I can write a speech.	1	2	3	4	_____

Reflection

Wow! You've finished Stand Out! You should be very proud of yourself. Remember, your learning doesn't stop just because you've finished this book. Learning is something that will continue for the rest of your life. And the skills that you've learned in this course will help you Stand Out in everything you do.
Good luck!

Stand Out 4 Vocabulary List

Pre-Unit
Learning strategies
conclusion sentence P5
draft P4
edit P4
errors P4
paragraph P4
strategies P3
support sentence P5
topic sentence P5
version P5
word family P6

Unit 1
Goals
achieve 6
advice 9
architect 4
brainstorm 6
counseling 9
determination 13
firm 4
immigrant 4
influence 13
intern 5
obstacle 6
overcome 6
partner 5
patience 13
qualifications 4
raise (a family) 4
retired 4
solution 6
suburban 4
surgeon 4
Time management
accomplish 15
allocate 15
burned out 16
combine 16
deadlines 16
effectively 16
organized 15
prioritize 16
realistic 15
sacrifice 15
schedule 15
set (a deadline) 16
simultaneously 16
urgency 16

Unit 2
Budgets
calculate 21
expenses 21
finances 21
spend 21
utilities 21
Making a purchase
bargain 23
clearance 23
consumer 23
guarantee 23
merchandise 23
merchant 23
pricing policy 23
purchase 23
refund 23
return 23
shipping costs 23
warranty 23
Credit cards
annual fee 28
application 27
apply 28
APR (annual percentage rate) 28
assets 28
bill 28
billing date 28
borrow 28
capacity 28
cash advance 28
character 28
charge 28
collateral 28
credit limit 28
creditworthiness 28
creditworthy 28
debit card 28
fixed rate 28
grace period 28
interest 28
introductory rate 28
issuer 28
late fee 28
payment 28
penalty 28
rebate 28
terminate 28
variable rate 28
Loans
afford 30
approve 30

credit check 30
deposit 30
down payment 30
financial commitment 30
financial planner 30
mortgage 30
purchase price 30

Unit 3
Housing
amenities 41
asking price 41
brand new 41
cozy 41
downtown 41
fireplace 41
ideal 45
location 41
market 41
master suite 41
negotiate 41
neighborhood 41
offer 41
price range 50
property 50
real estate agent 48
secluded 41
spacious 44
spectacular 41
suburban 41
view 41
Buying a home
assessor 55
closing 55
contract 56
cost comparison 55
debt 55
defect 56
first-time buyer 55
homebuyer 55
income 55
inspect 56
lender 55
motivation 55
upgrade 56

Unit 4
Community
bulletin board 66
community organization 73
literacy program 68
local government 61
recreation 61

transportation 61
visitor's guide 75
volunteer 68
Road maps
campground 70
freeway 70
highway 70
interstate 70
rest area 70
scenic 70

Unit 5
Health
bronchitis 83
chiropractor 87
cholesterol 86
floss 87
gums 87
junk food 86
muscle spasm 83
obstetrician 87
pediatrician 87
podiatrist 87
prenatal classes 87
Health insurance
co-pay 88
deductible 88
dental coverage 88
dependent 88
physician 89
pregnant 89
premium 88
prescription plan 88
provider 88
treatment 89
Nutrition
calories 90
carbohydrate 90
fiber 90
ingredients 90
protein 90
serving 90
sodium 90
vitamins 90
Medicines and illness
allergy 94
antibiotics 92
direction 93
discharge 94
dizziness 93
drowsiness 93
gargle 94
impair 93
indication 93
infection 94
non-prescription drugs 92
overdose 93

prescription drugs 92
prevent 94
relieve 93
respiratory 94
sneeze 94
symptom 93
virus 94
warning 93

Unit 6
Job skills
count on 102
detail-oriented 101
efficient 101
flexible 101
hard-working 101
open-minded 101
patient 101
responsible 101
self-motivated 101
well-organized 101
Jobs
accountant 103
administrative assistant 103
assembler 103
award 110
busboy 103
cashier 108
certificate 110
computer technician 103
conflict 114
cover letter 112
homemaker 103
interview 114
letter of recommendation 110
postal worker 103
references 109
resume 109
security guard 103
transcript 110

Unit 7
Workplace behavior
affect (be affected by a decision) 130
clarify 126
ethical 130
ethics 130
face (a problem) 130
get someone's attention 126
grooming 122
moral 130
offer 126
outcome 130
relevant 130
solve 126
suggest 126
take action 126

Asking for a raise
consider 136
contribution 132
counter (an objection) 132
counterpart 132
deserve 136
efficiency 136
field 132
flex time 132
formal 132
hectic 132
hesitate 135
illustrate 132
implement 136
increase 136
indispensable 132
procedures 134
productivity 134
set (a goal) 132
shift 136
train 136

Unit 8
Civic responsibility
accuse (be accused of a crime) 145
car registration 141
citizen 145
crime 145
driver's license 141
jaywalking 142
judge 145
juror 145
jury 145
jury summons 141
traffic ticket 141
resident 145
trial 145
Income tax
deduction 148
exemption 147
file (a tax return) 147
filing status 147
income 147
joint return 147
owe 147
refund 147
spouse 147
tax return 147
tax table 149
withhold 147
Elections
agenda 155
announce 151
ballot 151
campaign 150
candidate 150
city council 150

elect (be elected mayor) 151　　　lower 155　　　　　　　　　　proud 155
encourage 155　　　　　　　　　mayor 150　　　　　　　　　reduce 158
get involved in 157　　　　　　　nominate (be nominated for a　　run for (a position) 150
increase 156　　　　　　　　　　position) 150　　　　　　　　step down 150
invest 155　　　　　　　　　　　overcrowded 155　　　　　　　term 150
involve 156　　　　　　　　　　position 150　　　　　　　　　voice (an opinion) 150
local election 150　　　　　　　　protect 156　　　　　　　　　vote 150

Explanation of vocabulary used on income tax forms on page 147

dependent	person you support financially
exemption	amount of your income that won't be taxed. Each exemption represents an amount of money deducted from your taxable income for various reasons, such as number of dependents or disabilities.
file (verb)	send in a completed tax return
income	money earned from working or investments
joint return	when husband and wife declare their income together on the same form
overpaid	when too much tax was withheld by your employer during the year
owe (verb)	you need to pay more tax than the amount that was withheld
refund (noun)	amount of money that will be paid back to you by the government
spouse	husband or wife
tax return	form you fill out to declare your income each year and the federal or state tax you owe
W2 form	a form that your employer gives you to fill out for withholding payroll tax
withhold (verb)	deduct money from your paycheck

Stand Out 4 Irregular Verb List
The following verbs are used in *Stand Out 4* and have irregular past tense forms.

Base form	Simple past	Past participle	Base form	Simple past	Past participle	Base form	Simple past	Past participle
be	was, were	been	give	gave	given	sell	sold	sold
become	became	become	go	went	gone	send	sent	sent
begin	began	begun	grow	grew	grown	set	set	set
break	broke	broken	have	had	had	show	showed	showed/ shown
bring	brought	brought	hold	held	held	sit	sat	sat
build	built	built	hurt	hurt	hurt	sleep	slept	slept
buy	bought	bought	keep	kept	kept	speak	spoke	spoken
catch	caught	caught	know	knew	known	spend	spent	spent
come	came	come	learn	learned	learned/ learnt	spread	spread	spread
cost	cost	cost	lend	lent	lent	stand	stood	stood
do	did	done	lose	lost	lost	steal	stole	stolen
drink	drank	drunk	make	made	made	take	took	taken
drive	drove	driven	mean	meant	meant	teach	taught	taught
eat	ate	eaten	meet	met	met	tell	told	told
fall	fell	fallen	pay	paid	paid	think	thought	thought
feel	felt	felt	put	put	put	throw	threw	thrown
fight	fought	fought	read	read	read	wake	woke	woken
find	found	found	ride	rode	ridden	wear	wore	worn
fly	flew	flown	run	ran	ran	win	won	won
get	got	gotten	say	said	said	write	wrote	written

Used to

	Subject		*used to* + base verb	Object
	I		used to be	an architect.
	She	didn't	use to play	the piano.
Where	did they		use to live?	
Did	they		use to work	in a restaurant?

Used to + *base verb* expresses a past habit or state that is now different.

Adjective Clauses

	Main clause	Relative pronoun	Adjective clause
Subject clause	This is the *place*	where	I grew up.
	She is the *person*	who	influenced me most.
	A journal is *something*	that (which)	can help you focus on important things.
Object clause	This is the *woman*	who (whom)	I met yesterday.
	Here is the *book*	that (which)	you bought this morning.

Adjective clauses describe the preceding noun. They can describe a subject noun or an object noun. If the noun being described is an object, the relative pronoun can be left out.

Restrictive and Non-Restrictive Adjective Clauses

Restrictive adjective clauses	A homemaker is a person *who maintains a home and a family.* I applied for the job *that (which) was in the paper on Sunday.*	*Restrictive adjective clauses* give essential information about the noun they refer to. They cannot be omitted without losing the meaning of the sentence. They do not need commas.
Non-restrictive adjective clauses	My brother-in-law, *who owns his own business,* works very hard. I quit my job, *which I never really liked anyway.*	*Non-restrictive adjective clauses* give extra non-essential information about the noun they refer to. They can be omitted. They need commas.

Contrary-to-fact Conditionals

Condition (*if* + past tense verb)	Result (*would* + base verb)
If she *got* a raise,	she *would buy* a new house.
If they *didn't spend* so much money on rent,	they *would have* more money for entertainment.
If I *were* a millionaire,	I'*d give* all my money to charity.
If John *weren't* so busy at work,	he *would spend* more time with his children.

Question forms

If you *won* the lottery,	what *would* you *do?*
If you *won* the lottery,	*would* you *give up* your job?

Contrary-to-fact (or unreal) conditional statements are sentences that are not true. The *if*-clause can come in the first or second part of the sentence. In written English, use *were* (instead of *was*) for *if*-clauses with first- and third-person singular forms of *be*.

Questions with Comparative and Superlative Forms

Question word	Subject	Verb	Comparative or superlative form	Answer
Which	one	is	*bigger?*	The condominium.
	place		*the closest* to work?	The condominium *is bigger.*
	house	has	*more* rooms?	The condominium *is bigger*
	Ø		*the biggest* floor plan?	*than* the house.

Embedded Questions

Introductory question	Embedded question	Rule
Can you show me	where *Orange Avenue* <u>is</u>?	In an embedded question, the subject comes before the verb.
Do you know	*if* there <u>is</u> a library near here?	For *yes/no* questions, use *if* before the embedded question.
Could you tell me	when the library <u>opens</u>?	For questions with *do*, take out *do* or *does* and use the normal form of the verb.

Grammar Reference

Present Perfect

Subject	*have*	Past participle	Point or period of time	Sentence
I	have	studied	for three months / since April	I have studied English for three months / since April.
She	hasn't	visited	for a long time / since last year	She hasn't visited the dentist for a long time / since last year.
Question word	*have*	**Subject**	**Past participle**	**Question**
How long	have	they	worked	How long have they worked here?

Use *present perfect* to describe an action that happened in the past and continues in the present, when something happened more than once in the past (and could possibly happen again in the future), or for something that happened at an unspecified time in the past.

Present Perfect Continuous

Subject	*have*	*been*	Present participle	Sentence
I	have	been	studying	I have been studying for three months / since April.
She	hasn't	been	working	She hasn't been working long.
Question word	*have*	**Subject**	*been*	**Present participle**
How long	have	they	been	waiting?

Use *present perfect continuous* to emphasize the duration of an activity or state that started in the past and continues in the present or to show that an activity has been in progress recently. **Note:** Some verbs are not usually used in the continuous form, such as *be, believe, hate, have, know, like,* and *want*.

Past Perfect

Subject	*had*	Past participle	Example sentence
I, you, he, she, it, you, we, they	had	lived	He had lived in India before he came to the United States.

When describing two events that happened in the past, use *past perfect* for the event that happened first.

Passive Voice

Passive subject	*be*	Past participle	(*by* + person or thing)	Sentence
It	was	written	by Jim	The note was written by Jim.
They	were	sent	(by unknown person)	The orders were sent yesterday.

Use *passive voice* to emphasize the object of the action or when the doer of the action is unknown or unimportant. To make an active sentence into a passive sentence, switch the subject and the object and then change the verb to the correct tense of *be* + past participle. The word *by* is used before the doer of the action.

Passive Modals

Passive subject	Modal	*be*	Past participle	Sentence
Schools	should	be	built	More schools should be built.
Taxes	need to	be	increased	Taxes need to be increased.
Children	must	be	protected	Children must be protected.
Parents	have to	be	involved	Parents have to be involved.

Question Tags

Positive statement	Tag	Negative statement	Tag
She works,	doesn't she?	She doesn't work,	does she?
They can type,	can't they?	You won't apply,	will you?

A *question tag* makes a sentence into a question. Negative tags follow positive statements. Positive tags follow negative statements. For main verbs, use the verb *do* in the tag. For *be* and modal verbs, repeat the verb in the tag. Use question tags to check if something is true or to ask for agreement.

Unit 1

p. 1, Lesson 1, exercises A and C
Bita: Excuse me. Is this Ms. Johnson's ESL class? I'm new here.
Satoru: I'm new here, too. But I'm pretty sure this is her class. I used to attend this school five years ago, and this is where her class was.
Bita: Oh good. I used to go to school in the daytime before I got a new job. Now that I'm working during the day, I have to go to school at night. My other school doesn't offer night classes, so I had to leave there and come here.
Satoru: I used to go to school during the daytime too, but sometimes I take care of my grandchildren, so night classes are better for me. What kind of work do you do?
Bita: I used to be an architect in Iran. But I don't have the right qualifications to be an architect in the United States. So I'm doing administrative work for an engineering company until my English is good enough to go back to college and get the right degree.
Satoru: Wow, I'm impressed.
Bita: Do you work?
Satoru: Not any more. I used to work for a computer company, assembling computers, but now I just go to school and help my children with their children.
Bita: That's nice. I bet your children appreciate that. Why are you studying English?
Satoru: First of all, I want to help my grandchildren with their homework. But also, I figure since I live in this country, I should be able to speak the language. Don't you agree?
Bita: Completely!

p. 5, Lesson 2, exercise F
Yoshiko: How long do you think it will take you to become an architect?
Bita: My goal is to become a partner in a firm by the year 2010.
Yoshiko: What'll you do first?
Bita: Well, the first thing I have to do is improve my English, which I plan to study for two more years. Then by fall of 2004, I'll be ready to register for college.
Yoshiko: How long will it take you to finish?
Bita: Well, usually a degree in architecture takes five or six years to complete, but some of the classes I took in my country will transfer, so I should be able to do it faster. I plan to get my degree in the spring of 2008.
Yoshiko: Then you can become an architect?
Bita: Not quite. Then I'll have to become an intern to get some practical experience and prepare for my licensing exams.
Yoshiko: Exams?
Bita: Yes, I'll have to take a series of tests before I can get my license to be an architect. Once I have my license, which I hope to get in the winter of 2009, I can apply to work as a partner in an architectural firm.
Yoshiko: Shew! That sounds like a lot of work!
Bita: It will be. But it'll be worth it in the end.

p. 9, Lesson 4, exercise C
Conversation 1:
Anna: How's Harry doing these days?
Miyuki: I don't know what to do about him. He can't seem to settle down. He's angry all the time and is always fighting with the other students. My husband has to go and talk to the principal almost every week.
Anna: How about talking to the guidance counselor?
Miyuki: I've tried that but he doesn't have any suggestions.
Anna: Why don't you go and observe some classes and get to know the teachers better. Maybe that would help.
Miyuki: Yes, that's a great idea.

Conversation 2:
Ron: What am I going to do? My new landlord doesn't like dogs and he wants me to get rid of Herbie!
Mike: You can't do that! Has he met Herbie? Does he know what a polite friendly dog he is? Did you try introducing them?
Ron: No, that won't work. I don't think he likes any dogs….
Mike: Ok, then why don't you start looking for another apartment?

Conversation 3:
Sue: How's your back these days Patty?
Patty: It's getting worse. I'm going to need an operation. But I don't have any insurance.
Sue: I guess you'll have to save up some money then.
Patty: Yes, it could get expensive.
Sue: Or how about finding a job that gives you health insurance?
Patty: Yes, that's what I'll have to do.

Unit 2

p. 21, Lesson 1, exercise B
Todd: I think it's time we sat down and made a family budget. As the kids grow older, we're going to need to budget our money more wisely.
Sara: Good idea. How should we start?
Todd: Well, let's make a list of everything we spend money on and then let's guess at how much we spend in each category. Then we'll save our receipts for the next month and see how much we actually spent.
Sara: OK, why don't we start with the cars? Since both of them are paid off, we don't have any loan payments, but we do have to pay for gas, insurance, and maintenance. I'd say we spend $200 a month on gas, $150 a month on insurance, and I don't know about maintenance, but it might come to $450 a month for everything.
Todd: That sounds right. Now let's talk about utilities. Rent is $1500 a month. I know that for sure!
Sara: Yeah, and I'd say we spend about $40 on gas, $100 on electricity, and $20 on water. That adds up to $160.
Todd: Don't forget cable, phone, and Internet. Cable is $50, phone $80, and Internet $30. That's $160 right there.
Sara: Wow, we spend money on a lot of things!
Todd: And we're not even finished! How much do you think we spend on food each month?
Sara: I spend about $400 a month on groceries and I'd say we spend about $200 going out to dinner.
Todd: What about school supplies and clothing?
Sara: School supplies could be about $60 a month and clothing about $200.
Todd: Are we forgetting anything? . . . oh, medical expenses. It's a good thing we have insurance, but it doesn't pay for everything. I'd say we spend about $50 a month.
Sara: That sounds about right. And don't forget entertainment. Movies and taking the kids on trips soon adds up! I'd be willing to bet we spend at least $150 a month on those kinds of things—I'm afraid to add all this up!

p. 22, Lesson 1, exercise E
Sara: I can't believe it's been a month since we sat down and wrote down our budget. Time flies!
Todd: Yep, it sure does. OK, since we've already totaled up the receipts, let's write down the total amount of money we spent last month in each category.
Sara: OK, I've got the auto expenses. We spent $212.43 on gas, $150 on insurance, and nothing on maintenance, so that's $362.43 total. That's less than what we thought.

Todd: OK, rent and utilities. Obviously, rent is what we thought, $1500. Gas was $35.76, electricity was $150.02, and water was $22.34. That comes to $208.12. We were close on gas and water, but we were way off on the electricity.

Sara: I guess we're not used to that rate increase yet.

Todd: I don't think I'll ever get used to it. OK, cable was $50, phone was $155.72, and Internet was $30. That adds up to $235.72.

Sara: Not bad. I guess the bigger phone bill was because of all those calls you made to your mother last month. Maybe we can make her pay for it!

Todd: Oh, she'd love that! OK, what else?

Sara: I spent $359.81 last month on groceries and we spent about $300 going out to dinner. I guess we underestimated that one.

Todd: What about school supplies and clothing?

Sara: School supplies were about $30, clothing was $102.14. But I still think we should leave the clothing budget at $200 because the boys will be growing and need new clothes quite often.

Todd: Good idea. We spent $45.28 on medical expenses and $132.96 on entertainment.

Sara: All right. Let's add it up!

p. 30, Lesson 5, exercises A, B, C, and D

Part 1:

Todd: I really appreciate you taking time to talk to me.

Financial Planner: No problem, Todd.

Todd: Well, as I told you over the phone, the boys are starting to grow up and Sara and I would like to move into a permanent place of our own. We're just a little worried about how we're going to pay for it.

Fin. Planner: I think it's great that you and Sara are ready to take the next step. But only you can decide if you're ready to buy a house. Here's what I tell all my clients. First, you have to ask yourself three questions. Do you have money set aside for a down payment? Do you have enough money each month to make a loan payment? And are you ready to make a long-term financial commitment? If you can answer yes to all three of those questions, you are ready to buy a home.

Part 2:

Todd: How much will we need for a down payment?

Fin. Planner: Well, that all depends on how much the house is that you want to buy. Also, you have to decide how much you want to put down. It's best if you can put 20% down, but some people can only put 5% down. The more you put down, the lower your monthly payments will be.

Todd: OK, so if we can answer yes to all of those questions, what's the next step?

Fin. Planner: First you need to determine how much you can afford to spend on a house. Next, you get approved for a loan of that amount. Third, start looking for a home in your price range. And fourth, make an offer on the house you want.

Todd: Looking for a home and making an offer are easy. But how do we figure out how much we can afford?

Fin. Planner: The best thing to do is gather all the necessary paperwork and then we can determine how much you can spend.

Part 3:

Todd: What's the necessary paperwork?

Fin. Planner: I'll need six things. I'll need your social security number to run a credit check, tax statements from the past two years, two of your most recent pay stubs, the most recent statements from all your bank accounts, your most recent credit card statements, and statements from any other loans

that you have. Once I have those things, I should be able to determine what your purchase price can be. If not, I'll ask you for more information.

Todd: Is there anything else I need to know?

Fin. Planner: That's it for now. Why don't you and Sara sit down and discuss the three questions we talked about. If the answer is yes to all three, start gathering that paperwork and give me a call.

Todd: Great! Thanks for all your help, Jim.

Unit 3

p. 43, Lesson 2, exercise A

Courtney: I went and looked at houses yesterday.

Joey: You did? How did it go?

Courtney: Well, I found two that I really liked. One was a three-bedroom house and the other was a two-bedroom condominium.

Joey: Which one did you like better?

Courtney: Well they both have their plusses and minuses. The house is closer to my job than the condo. But the condo is in a much nicer neighborhood.

Joey: What about price?

Courtney: The condo is cheaper than the house but the condo has association fees.

Joey: Did you talk to any of the people who live in the area?

Courtney: Yep. I met one of the women who lives in the condominium complex and she looked in both neighborhoods as well when she was buying her place. She said the condominium complex is safer than the housing neighborhood because of the gate at the front. She also said that there are more children in the complex and that the neighbors seem to be friendlier because everyone lives so close together.

p. 47, Lesson 3, exercise G

Home 1

Wanna live like a king? Then you can't pass up the Prince's Palace. Offered at a mere 1.2 million, this sprawling 15,000 square foot palace is located at the top of a hill far away from other residences. Not only does it have every appliance you can think of, but all the rooms have beautiful hardwood floors. Wanna find out more about this princely estate? Call today!

Home 2

Always wanted to take a house and make it your own? Here's your chance! Settle into this four-bedroom, 2,000 square foot Fixer-Upper for only $150,000. Located in a busy neighborhood with lots of other families, this place is perfect for a young family.

Home 3

Move out of the slow life and into the fast lane! A beautifully spacious 1,000 square foot studio apartment at the top of one of the city's newest high-rises is just what you're looking for. The building has 24-hour security. Utility room with washers and dryers is in the basement. The owner wants to lease it for $2000 a month but is willing to sell. Hurry! This one will go fast!

Home 4

You've finally decided it's time to move out of the city and into the country. Well, we've got the place for you. This three-bedroom rural residence is just what you need. It's a spacious 3,500 square foot ranch-style home with a huge back yard and a pool. It's located at the end of cul-de-sac where there are only five other homes. It is now being offered at $125,000.

Unit 4

p. 66, Lesson 3, exercise D
1. I want to do individual exercises that will help me relax.
2. I've always wanted to learn how to play an instrument.
3. I need a place to send my kids for the summer while I'm at work.
4. Wouldn't it be fun to play on a team with other people?
5. There's gotta be something my grandmother can do Sunday nights to keep herself busy.
6. I need to find a place to live.
7. Is there a gym around here where I can play basketball?
8. I've always wanted to learn some crafts.
9. Have you seen my cat?

p. 71, Lesson 5, exercise D
1. Since you'll be coming from Rose, get on 24 going west. Then take 315 South. You'll drive for a while and then get off at the first exit.
2. From Grandville, get on 315 South. Then take 24 East. You'll pass the airport. Get off right before 24 and 89 intersect.
3. If you're coming from Poppington, take 315 North. Then get on 13 West, the scenic route, and go on to 15 North. You'll pass by Lake Ellie, which might be a nice place to stop and have lunch. Then continue on 15 North till you get to 315 North. Take the first exit.
4. From Rose, take 89 South until you get to the first exit. Keep going till you get to the hospital.

Unit 5

p. 86, Lesson 3, exercise A
Doctor: Rosa, I can give you some more tests, but you'll have to come back in two weeks to get the results. Here's an information leaflet that tells you about exercises that will be good for your back and for your knees. If you do more exercise, your cholesterol should go down. The fact is, if you don't stop eating junk food, you'll have serious health problems. The most important thing is to stay active.

p. 86, Lesson 3, exercise B
Friend: What did the doctor tell you, Rosa?
Rosa: She said she could give me some more tests.
Friend: Why? Are you very sick?
Rosa: Not now, but I might get sick. The doctor told me the most important thing was to stay active. She told me if I did more exercise, my cholesterol should go down.
She said if I didn't stop eating junk food, I would have serious health problems. She said I would have to come back in two weeks.

Unit 6

p. 102, Lesson 1, exercise E
1. My name is Lam and I love to be outdoors. I'm a hard worker and like to work with my hands. I don't like to tell other people what to do, but I don't mind taking orders from my boss.
2. Hello, I'm Lilia and I love working with people. I'm very customer service oriented and like to help people. I wouldn't make a good cashier because I'm not very good with numbers. But I'm willing to work hard and I learn quickly.
3. My name is Morteza and I was an engineer in my country. Unfortunately, I don't have the right qualifications to do that here, but I'm very good at technical things. I know a lot about computers and really like working with them. I prefer to work alone because I'm not very good with people.
4. Hi, I'm Hilda. I've never had a job before but I'm very organized and good with details. I've always taken care of the finances at our house, so I'm good with numbers. Also, I'm creative and like to come up with new ideas.

Unit 7

p. 129, Lesson 4, exercise D
1. He sent the package yesterday, didn't he?
2. We'll get our paychecks tomorrow, won't we?
3. They didn't unload those boxes yet, did they?
4. Martina hasn't ever assembled computers, has she?
5. You're just learning about tag questions, aren't you?

Unit 8

p. 143, Lesson 2, exercise B
Bita: Is this Consuela?
Consuela: Yes. Who's this?
Bita: This is Bita from Bellingham, Washington.
Consuela: Hi! How are you doing?
Bita: I'm OK. A little busy with work and school but I'm surviving. Hey, I was wondering if you could help me with something.
Consuela: Of course! What do you need?
Bita: Well, I think it's time for me to get a driver's license. Public transportation is taking up too much of my time and I need to be able to get around faster. I've been saving up to buy a car but I still have to get my license. And I remember the other day that you said you had gotten your license and registered your car, so I thought maybe you could give me some advice.
Consuela: Sure I can.
Bita: Well, I already have my driver's license from Iran. Do I still have to take the test?
Consuela: Yes, you'll have to take the written test and the driving test. Only people from other states in the United States can get the driving test waived.
Bita: OK, so how do I prepare for the written test?
Consuela: First, you need to go to the DMV and get a Driver's Handbook to study the rules of the road for the written test.
Bita: How many questions are on the test?
Consuela: In California, the written test has 36 questions. In Washington, it may be different.
Bita: How many questions do I have to get correct? And what if I don't pass it the first time?
Consuela: You can miss five. But you have three chances to pass the test, so if you don't pass the first time you can take it two more times.
Bita: OK. What about the driving test?
Consuela: First, you need to make an appointment. They won't let you test without one. Second, a licensed driver must accompany you to the DMV in the car that you'll use to take the test.
Bita: And then they test me on my driving skills?
Consuela: Yep.
Bita: That should be easy. I've been practicing with my brother for over a year. So how do I apply for the license?
Consuela: First, you have to get an application and fill it out. Then you have to take the application to the DMV.
Bita: OK, so what do I have to do next?
Consuela: Well, you have to take the written test, take a vision exam, show them proof of your social security number and your date of birth, give them your thumbprint, and have your picture taken.
Bita: How much does that cost?
Consuela: $12.
Bita: OK, I think I can do this.
Consuela: I know you can. Good luck! Call me and let me know how it goes.
Bita: I sure will. Thanks a lot, Consuela!
Consuela: Any time.

p. 154, Lesson 7, exercise A

Antonio Juliana: First of all, I want to thank you all for coming today. It is my pleasure to speak to you and I hope that you will vote for me come election day. I'll be brief and to the point. My biggest concern is our streets. There is too much gang violence and I want to wipe it out. I think we can start by getting our children off the streets and taking care of the homeless people. It's time for us to regain our streets and feel safe again. Once this happens we can focus on other problems like overcrowded schools and our public transportation system. I know you have a tough decision to make but I hope that when you go to the polls next Tuesday, you'll put a check next to my name, Antonio Juliana.

Gary Hurt: I have been waiting for this day. A day when I could appear before you and tell you what I'm going to do if elected. These are not empty promises but things that WILL HAPPEN if you elect Gary Hurt as your mayor. The environment will be my number one priority. Our beaches will be clean again. Our public transportation system will be so good that you won't want to drive your cars anymore. I will use your tax dollars to create more parks and safe places for our children to play. Our city will be great once again if you vote for Gary Hurt!

Kwan Tan: Good evening and thank you for coming tonight! This community has given me so many opportunities and, in running for mayor, I hope to give something back to the city that welcomed me as an immigrant, educated me through my teen years, and supported me as I opened my first business.

First on my agenda is education. I will make sure your tax dollars are used to build more schools, so our children won't have to sit in overcrowded classrooms. I'll lower the tuition at our community colleges, so all of us will have a chance to continue our education. I'll implement standards to ensure that schools are teaching our kids what they need to know. I'll start a parent-teacher program that encourages parents to participate actively in their kids' schools. Our children are the future of our community and we should invest time and money in their success.

Vote for me on Election Day and you'll have schools and a community to be proud of!

Example summary of article *The Common Cold,* Unit 5, Lesson 7, page 95

The article *The Common Cold,* published by The National Institute of Allergy and Infectious Diseases (NIAID) in 1996, describes the causes, symptoms, prevention, and treatment of the common cold. The author states that colds are one of the most common illnesses in children and adults. The symptoms include difficulty in breathing, sneezing, sore throat, cough, and headache. Colds are spread by viruses that are present on things we touch and in the air we breathe. The article emphasizes that washing our hands and not touching our noses and mouths are two of the best ways to prevent catching a cold. The author points out that if we do get a cold, the only way to treat it is by relieving the symptoms: sleep, drinking lots of water, gargling with salt water, and taking aspirin for the headaches. Claims that vitamin C can help prevent colds have not been proven.

Stand Out 4 Skills Index

ACADEMIC SKILLS

Charts, tables, maps, and graphs, 2, 11, 21, 29, 46, 53–54, 63, 69, 70–72, 84, 86, 104, 122, 126, 128, 156

Charts, tables, maps, graphs, and diagrams, P6, 2, 4–5, 6, 7, 11, 21, 22, 29, 31, 33, 42, 44, 46, 49, 53–54, 63, 69, 70–72, 81–82, 84, 86, 104, 105, 106, 172

Grammar

Adjective clauses, 10–12, 18, 103–104, 118, 164

Adjectives

Comparative and superlative, 43–47, 164

Direct speech, 86–87, 97

Indirect speech, 86–87, 97

Pronouns, relative

who, which, where, 10–12

Questions

Embedded questions, 63–64, 76

Information questions, 48–50, 60

Tag questions, 128–129, 137, 140, 165

wh- questions, 2, 26

yes/no questions, 26, 28–50, 37, 60

Sequencing transitions, 151

Verbs

can, could, 7, 83–85, 97

Contrary-to-fact conditionals, 25–26

Indirect speech, 86-87

Irregular, 163

Passive modals, 154–156, 165

Passive voice, 123–124, 137, 165

Past perfect tense, 83–85, 97, 165

Present perfect continuous tense, 83–85, 97, 165

Present perfect tense, 165

Simple present tense, 3

used to, 1–3, 18, 164

Listening

Advertisements, 47

Announcements, 66

Conversations, 1, 5, 9, 21, 22, 30, 43, 45, 86, 124, 125, 143

Directions, 72, 77

Personal descriptions, 102

Questions, 129

Speeches, 154

Stories, 48

Mathematics

Distance estimates, 70

Expense calculations, 21–22

Travel time estimates, 71

Pronunciation

Stress and intonation, 20, 60, 140, 160

Word linking

contractions, 120

do, would, could, did, 80

he linked to previous word, 100

words ending in *w,* 40

Reading

Advertisements, 41, 57

Aloud, 2, 34, 57, 127

Articles, 55–56, 94, 132

Brochures, 68

Bulletin boards, 66

Charts, tables, maps, graphs, and diagrams, 2, 11, 21, 29, 46, 53–54, 63, 69, 70–72, 82, 84, 86, 104, 126, 128, 156

Comprehension, 15–16, 55–56, 91, 102

Conversations, 62, 65, 83, 123, 142, 145

Details, 90-91

Context clues, 4

Descriptions, 75

Flow charts, 150

Food labels, 90–91

Forms, 146, 147

Job descriptions, 113

Letters, 51, 136

Lists, P3, 73, 101

Main idea, 23

Medicine labels, 92–93

Paragraphs, P6, 4, 8, 10, 13, 28, 31, 122

Resumes, 109

Sentences, 87

Sequence of events, 55, 108

Skimming and scanning, 88

Speeches, 155

Stories, 48, 107, 134

Speaking

Class/group discussion, 6, 27, 29, 31, 32, 33, 37, 45, 46, 47, 53, 54, 57, 68, 69, 73, 82, 85, 93, 94, 98, 101, 103, 110, 118, 121, 130, 131, 133, 135, 152

Conversations, 46, 83, 123, 134

Directions, 72

Discussions with teacher, 4, 23, 43, 145

Interviews and presentations, 114–116

Introductions, P2

Pair activities, 13, 31, 34, 44, 45, 47, 53, 56, 57, 62, 65, 67, 70, 72, 73, 74, 75, 89, 103, 104, 106, 114, 115, 125, 126, 130, 138, 142, 151

Questions

Answering, 4, 26, 35, 45–47, 49, 50, 69, 85, 107, 123, 125

Asking, 1, 26, 37, 45–47, 62, 69, 73, 74, 75, 77, 142

Vocabulary, P4–P5, 30, 32, 36, 42, 49, 50, 53, 56, 57, 87, 90, 93, 98, 130, 138, 141, 158

Context, 4, 16, 29, 48, 132–134, 145

Dictionary use, P6

Vocabulary cards, 17, 37, 57

Word families, P6, 98

Word list, 161–163

Writing

Brainstorming, 7, 13

Charts, tables, maps, graphs, and diagrams, P6, 4–5, 6, 7, 22, 31, 33, 42, 44, 49, 54, 81–82, 105, 106, 122

Conversations, 8, 18, 34

Descriptions, 76, 77, 131

Editing, P4–P5, 14

Forms, P2, 27, 88–89, 116, 144, 146, 147–149

Goals, 4

Letters

Business letters, 35–36, 51–52, 136, 152–153

Cover letters, 112–113

Lists, P3, 1, 15, 21, 24, 30, 31, 38, 50, 51, 52, 61, 64, 73, 74, 75, 78, 81, 82, 92, 102, 105, 106, 107, 110, 117, 135, 138, 142, 152, 158

Paragraphs, 12, 13–14, 151

Prewriting activities, 13

Punctuation, P4–P5

Questions, 33, 63, 77, 129

Resumes, 109, 111

Sentences, P5, 2, 3, 11, 12, 18, 26, 48, 53, 95, 104, 108, 155, 156, 158

Conclusion sentences, 14

Conditional statements, 37

Indirect statements, 87

Summaries, 94, 95, 96

Support sentences, 14

Topic sentences, 13, 14

Speeches, 156

Titles, 14

LEARNER LOGS

20, 40, 60, 80, 100, 120, 140, 160

LIFE SKILLS

Consumer Education
Advertisements, 24, 32–33, 38
Complaints, 34–36
Housing purchases, 41–80
Internet, 23, 24, 33
Purchase process, 24, 38, 39

Government and Community Resources
Educational opportunities, accessing, P2
Elections, 150–151, 154–156, 159
Income tax, 147–149
Jury duty, 145–146
Locating and accessing community services, P2, 61–72, 75–79
Solving community problems, 141–142, 152–153, 157
Volunteering, 73–74

Health and Nutrition
Common cold, 94–96
Doctor visits, 83, 86–87
Food labels, 90–91
Health habits, 81–82
Insurance forms, 88–89
Medicine labels, 92–93
Personal hygiene and grooming, 122

Interpersonal Communication
Advice, giving and responding to, 8–9, 18
Problem/solution identification and explanation, 6–7, 18

Time and Money
Budget planning, 21–22, 38

Credit cards, 27–29
Loans, 30–31
Time zones, 172

Transportation and Travel
Drivers' licenses, 143–144
Map reading, 70–72

TEAM PROJECTS
19, 39, 59, 79, 99, 119, 139, 159

TOPICS
Advertising, 32–33, 41–42, 47, 57
Advice, 8–9
Budgeting, 21–22, 38
Civic responsibility, 141–160
College admission applications, P2
Community resources, 61–80
Consumer complaints, 34–36
Credit cards, 27–29
Drivers' licenses, 143–144
Elections, 150–151, 154–156, 159
Ethics in workplace, 130–131
Goals, 4–5, 19
Health, 81–100
Housing purchases, 41–80
Income tax, 147–149
Job applications, 109–113, 119
Job interviews, 114–116
Job searches, 105–106
Job skills, 101–102
Job titles and responsibilities, 103–104, 107–108
Jury duty, 145–146
Learning strategies, P3, 158
Libraries, 68–69
Loans, 30–31
Map reading, 70–72

Medicine, 92–93
Nutrition, 90–91
Obstacles and solutions, 6–7
People, 13–14
Processes, 24, 38, 39, 55–56
Shopping, 23–24, 38, 39
Study strategies, P3
Time management, 15–16
Volunteering, 73–74
Women at work, 132–134
Workplace behavior, 121–140

WORKFORCE DEVELOPMENT SKILLS

Maintaining Employment
Asking for a raise, 135–136
Communication with supervisors, 125–127
Problem solving skills, 139
Women at work, 132–134
Workplace behavior, 121–140
Workplace ethics, 130–131

Obtaining Employment
Job applications, resumes and letters, 109–113, 119
Job interviews, 114–116
Job searches, 105–106
Job titles and responsibilities, 103–104
Skills inventory, 101–102
Work experience, 107–108

Technology
Internet use, 9, 16, 23, 24, 29, 33, 42, 52, 62, 74, 76, 89, 91, 93, 105, 106, 111, 156

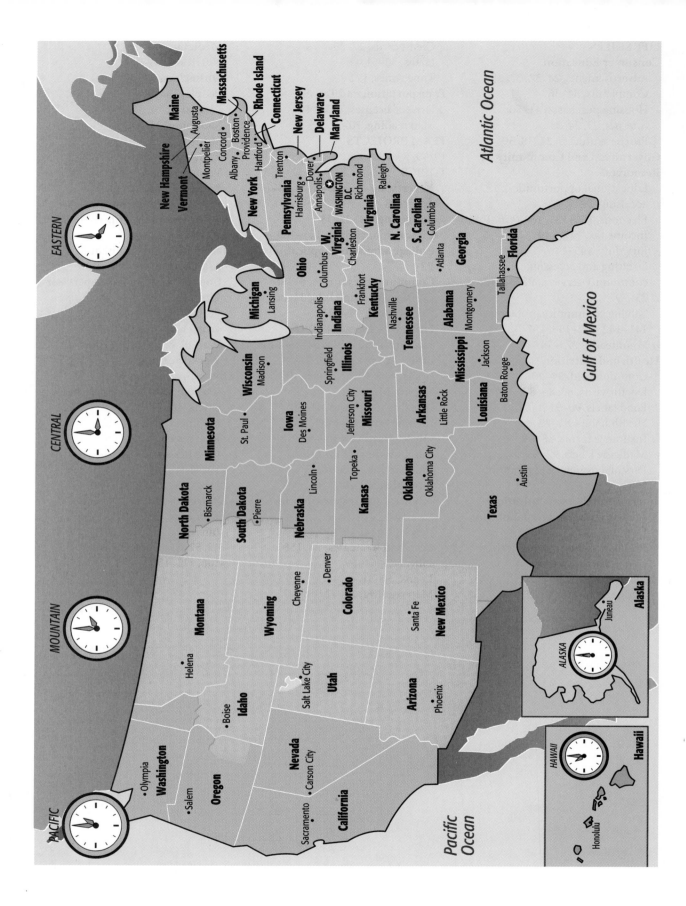

Atlantic Ocean

EASTERN

CENTRAL

MOUNTAIN

PACIFIC

Maine
Augusta
New Hampshire
Vermont
Montpelier
Concord
Massachusetts
Boston
Rhode Island
Providence
Connecticut
New Jersey
Delaware
Maryland
Albany
Hartford
Trenton
Dover
New York
Pennsylvania
Harrisburg
Annapolis
WASHINGTON D.C.
Richmond
Raleigh
Virginia
N. Carolina
Columbia
S. Carolina
W. Virginia
Charleston
Ohio
Columbus
Frankfort
Kentucky
Nashville
Tennessee
Atlanta
Georgia
Tallahassee
Florida
Alabama
Montgomery
Michigan
Lansing
Indianapolis
Indiana
Illinois
Springfield
Wisconsin
Madison
Mississippi
Jackson
Baton Rouge
Louisiana
Gulf of Mexico

Minnesota
St. Paul
Iowa
Des Moines
Jefferson City
Missouri
Little Rock
Arkansas

North Dakota
Bismarck
South Dakota
Pierre
Nebraska
Lincoln
Topeka
Kansas
Oklahoma
Oklahoma City
Austin

Montana
Helena
Wyoming
Cheyenne
Denver
Colorado
Santa Fe
New Mexico
Texas

Idaho
Boise
Salt Lake City
Utah
Arizona
Phoenix

Washington
Olympia
Oregon
Salem
Nevada
Carson City
Sacramento
California

Pacific Ocean

Alaska
Juneau
ALASKA

HAWAII
Hawaii
Honolulu

Map of the United States